D0919656

BOTH
SIDES
OF
THE
OCEAN

BOTH SIDES OF THE OCEAN

A Russian writer's travels in
Italy and the United States

BY VIKTOR NEKRASOV

Translated by
ELIAS KULUKUNDIS

HOLT, RINEHART AND WINSTON

NEW YORK · CHICAGO · SAN FRANCISCO

Translation and Introduction
Copyright © 1964
by Elias Kulukundis

All rights reserved,
including the right to
reproduce this book or portions
thereof in any form.

Published simultaneously
in Canada by Holt, Rinehart
and Winston of Canada, Limited.

Library of Congress
Catalog Card Number: 64-14354
First Edition

Design by Ulrich Ruchti
86008-0114
Printed in the
United States of America

TRANSLATOR'S FOREWORD

Viktor Nekrasov is fifty-two. He was born in Paris, lived there the first four years of his life, and then his family returned to the Ukraine where he has lived since then, in and around its capital Kiev. After a short experiment as an actor, he chose a career in architecture, and attended the Kiev Construction Institute where he received his training and a degree. He served in the Red Army from 1941 to 1945 and fought in the Battle of Stalingrad. In 1944, he became a member of the Communist party.

In 1946 he began to publish his writing. His first novel, *In the Trenches of Stalingrad,* won him a Stalin Prize in 1947 and immediately assured him success in his second profession. It was followed by two more novels, *Home Town* and *Second Night,* which consolidated his position in Soviet letters; and since then, with unusual breadth of interest, he has written with authority on literature and politics, painting, architecture and the contemporary film. His stories and articles have been regular features of *Novy Mir,* one of Soviet Russia's leading literary journals, ac-

68656

companying the work of such colleagues as Pasternak, Ehrenburg, Dudintsev, and Solzhenitsin.

Often our own experience makes it hard for us to understand the way the Soviet Union treats its writers. We may find it hard to believe, for example, that *Both Sides of the Ocean* was written in a country where thousands of people have assembled in stadiums to hear contemporary poetry read over loud-speakers, a country where works of literature, including the very issues of *Novy Mir* that featured it, can sell out editions totaling nearly a hundred thousand copies in a few days. And yet, what is really important in the Soviet Union is not how many people read a writer's work, but why they read it and why he writes.

Not everyone goes to these poetry readings just to hear poetry. Beside the romance and excitement of the spectacle, people might go simply to find out what is happening in the world, to keep up to date with the issues of the day.

The role of the writer is thus combined with the journalist and the publicist, the prose writer no less than the poet. Since the days when political writing was driven underground or beyond the borders by the Tsarist government, literature has been the most convenient vehicle for Russian social commentary. The Soviet reader, like his predecessor, turns to novels to find out the social ideas of the day. And Soviet novelists, like the great novelists of the Russian literary past, ignore these ideas at their peril.

Both Sides of the Ocean was written in a country where the writings of a group of intellectuals were translated into a political action that transformed the lives of 200 million people. No wonder then that the nation which emerged from this political action should number its writers among the most powerful of its citizens: that the government should have so confounded the purposes of art with the purposes of politics that the writer has become a writer-ideologist, accountable not only for artistic truth but political cohesion as well. No wonder, either, that Soviet cultural authorities constantly agitate about deluded or malicious writers infecting the Soviet people with a foreign ideology.

But this can only partly explain the way Viktor Nekrasov has been treated in his country.

In 1957, Nekrasov took his first trip to Western Europe, a privilege which every Soviet writer envies him much more than his Stalin Prize. It was his first mature encounter with Western life, but he came to it with a familiarity bred not only by his reading but by a French-speaking mother, who was educated in Switzerland. After this visit, he wrote his first book on Italy, *First Acquaintance*, and his work began to attract a wide readership in the West. It was followed by *Kira Georgievna*, a novel about a marriage divided by the husband's imprisonment in a Stalinist prison camp, his first to be translated into English. But more significantly, his *First Acquaintance* launched him in a genre he was to cultivate further: the literature of travel in the West.

In November, 1960, Nekrasov was sufficiently respected by his government to be one of sixteen Soviet citizens chosen to spend fourteen days in the United States. In March, 1962, he was invited to Florence to attend the second congress of the European Society of Writers. And these two experiences became *Both Sides of the Ocean*, a work which brought him Soviet readers anxious not only to be up to date with the issues of their own world, but to know what life is like beyond the Communist borders, even in the United States.

His travels were as much of a whirlwind as the book that came from them. People who saw Nekrasov in New York remember a lanky, youthful figure, striding the pavement with head tilted boyishly at the tops of skyscrapers: an angular face, a mischievous lock of black hair over the forehead, tiny mustache to match it, and unresting black eyes. They recall an open and generous nature, unreserved in the first meeting, rich in laughter and enthusiasm. Unmarried and without children himself, he responded with the wonder of a child, to the "Camel" smoker on Times Square, the shops and arcades of Broadway, and American trains and toys. And although he knew no English when he came to America, he had a mimic's ability surviving from his acting days and lost no chance to mouth the English words (as he lost no chance to include them in the Russian text): *Thirty-first Street, uptown, downtown.* People remember a mind impulsive in its movement, as quick to oppose as to befriend; a mercurial temperament; the child's impatience with anything in his way.

The book first appeared in November, 1962, in the same issue of *Novy Mir* that contained Solzhenitsin's *One Day in the Life of Ivan Denisovich*. At that time, Soviet critics were dividing their attention between Solzhenitsin's view of Stalinist prison life and Khrushchev's tantrum at the sight of "modernist" art at the Moscow Exhibition Hall. Perhaps for this reason, perhaps because the authorities hadn't decided how to react to it, *Both Sides of the Ocean* went unobserved in the Soviet press for a full two months after its publication.

Then, on January 20, 1963, *Izvestia* published a sharply worded editorial entitled *Tourist with a Walking Stick.* Nekrasov was attacked for superficiality, for erroneous generalization, for compromise toward what he saw, for "promoting peaceful coexistence in the field of ideology," for "bourgeois objectivism." Immediately, other reviewers followed *Izvestia's* lead and published their attacks in other newspapers. One critic even took time out during a review of another book about America to insert a hostile paragraph about Nekrasov. Then, on March 8, 1963, in a speech before writers, artists, and ideologists, Khrushchev chided Nekrasov for the first time, along with his colleagues Ehrenburg and Yevtushenko. After that, Nekrasov was asked to repudiate his errors at a meeting of writers and ideologists in the Ukraine. He stood his ground resolutely, denied the accusations, and declared that such an admission would be a loss of self-respect for a writer and a Communist. Then, at last, in a speech before the Plenum of the Central Committee on June 21, 1963, Khrushchev made his ominous suggestion that Nekrasov did not belong in the Communist party.

In its opening volley in January, *Izvestia* referred to the episode in which a Soviet journalist cautions Nekrasov to maintain a proportion of black and white when he writes about the United States, "a proportion of fifty-fifty." In *Both Sides of the Ocean* Nekrasov pointedly rejects this advice: far from endorsing such a formula, Nekrasov is pleading against any formula at all, against any stereotype. But according to *Izvestia,* Nekrasov accepts the journalist's advice without knowing it, and in doing so, he attempts what is supposedly impossible for a Soviet writer, to be objective about what he sees. According to Communist reasoning, since a writer is limited by his own point of view, he must ever identify himself with the point of view of the Communist party to avoid being led into error. If he refuses to do so, if he chooses to rely on the objectivity of his own judgment, he is guilty of "bourgeois objectivism." This was the basis of *Izvestia's* initial charge. Then later, as Nekrasov was called on to repudiate his errors, by an extension of the same reasoning he was being asked to admit that his firsthand account of America could be corrected by party ideologists who themselves had never seen America.

A second point of controversy is Nekrasov's attitude to art. His defense of Ucello in the Italian chapter is especially significant because Ucello is not highly considered in the Soviet Union, not nearly so highly as Vasari, whose opinion Nekrasov contradicts. Ucello's use of certain techniques were far advanced for his time and bring him uncomfortably close to the hated "modernists" of the bourgeois West. Nekrasov's treatment of Salvador Dali, furthermore, is obviously unsatisfactory: "[He's] frightening, incomprehensible, but by God [he's] entertaining." And his list of painters and sculptors in the Guggenheim Museum—"Cezanne, Modigliani, Leger, Picasso, Paul Klee, Kandinsky, Chagall, sculptures by Lipchitz and Brancusi"—must read to Soviet ideologists like a Miltonic catalogue of devils.

Still, on March 8, Khrushchev's attack on Nekrasov was a glancing blow, aimed at *Guard of Lenin,* a Soviet movie then scheduled for release which Nekrasov lauds in his American chapter. (After Khrushchev's speech the film was suspended for revisions, offending passages were altered or omitted, and the film once again was scheduled to appear.) Khrushchev singled out a scene, described by Nekrasov, in which a young Soviet worker appeals to the ghost of his father who was killed in the war. The young man turns to his father with the basic question of how he should live, but the father cannot answer him and disappears. Khrushchev's objection was pious and vehement: "Everyone knows that even animals do not abandon their young," he said. "Can it be imagined that a father would not answer his son's question and not help him with advice on how to find the

correct path in life?" According to Khrushchev, such a suggestion implies that there is a conflict of generations in
Soviet life, reminiscent of the 1840's and 60's which Tur-
genev dramatized in *Fathers and Sons*. The idea is another
bête noire which Soviet critics have spared no words to
exorcise, and we have the word of the arch-critic of them all
that at one time at least, this is what *Guard of Lenin* was all
about.

We cannot know just why *Both Sides of the Ocean* led
Khrushchev to urge Nekrasov's expulsion from the party.
In its editorial on July 5, 1963, the New York *Times* em-
phasized the weakness of Khrushchev's criticism. Many have
suggested that in attacking Nekrasov, Ehrenburg, Yevtushenko and the younger poets, Khrushchev was only doing
the bidding of Stalinists in the Kremlin. It is possible also
that Khrushchev may still have been hoping for reconcilia-
tion with the Chinese, in the "ideological talks" scheduled
for July. The June attack on Nekrasov, therefore, may have
been for the benefit of the Chinese (and Russian Stalinists
in sympathy with the Chinese position), a gesture to show
them what Khrushchev can do to a writer who has anything
good to say about the United States.

But these are only speculations. The fact remains that
after the failure of the July ideological talks, Khrushchev
did not carry out his threat of expelling Nekrasov. As
a member in good standing of the Communist party,
Nekrasov has gone on to write a set of French travel notes,
which *Novy Mir* expects to publish in 1964. In any case,
the attacks on Nekrasov were part of the cultural offensive
of 1963 aimed at the influence of "Western ideology" on
Soviet life, the corollary of Khrushchev's policy of peaceful
coexistence which attempts to draw the battle lines ever
sharper in the field of "ideology."

One reviewer complained that Nekrasov mentions twenty-story department stores when the tallest has only eleven. (He might have complained of other inaccuracies, such as Nekrasov's statement that New York City is the capital of the state, or his description of the Pennsylvania Railroad as serving mainly Pennsylvania, Ohio and Indiana.) But at other times, when it suited them, Nekrasov's critics were purposely inattentive to his text. Here are some examples of their comments, set against the appropriate passages:

> Nekrasov: . . . *in the two weeks I spent in America, I didn't make friends with a single American. . . . I can't help it. When I write about Americans, about their tastes and aspirations, about their likes and dislikes, I shall be writing at second hand. . . . But I can't help it.*

> Izvestia: *The writer himself admits that he saw too little, that in the United States he "did not get to know or make friends with a single American" and that therefore he was obliged even to invent things in his sketches. . . . He "saw too little" and "did not get to know" and yet he decided to write the sketches anyway.*

> Nekrasov: [*A Soviet journalist who was touring America with me told me once*] *"When are they going to show us the slums? . . . There's nothing to write about—everything is so slick, clean and comfortable." Somehow I don't want to be like him. . . . If that's all you want to see when you go to a foreign country,*

why go at all? I am always ashamed when I see people take pleasure in the misfortunes of others.

Komsomolskaya Pravda: *It is surprising, to put it mildly, what Viktor Nekrasov failed to see in the U.S.A.—the crying social contradictions, the unbridled reign of militarism, the McCarthyist hysteria. . . .*

Nekrasov: (*On the movie* Guard of Lenin) *I am endlessly grateful to [the authors] for not dragging in the old worker by his graying mustaches, the one who understands everything and always has exactly the right answer for anything you ask him. If he had come by with his instructive sayings, it would have ruined the picture.*

N. S. Khrushchev: *"And this is written by a Soviet writer in a Soviet magazine!"* (*Cries of "Shame!" in the audience*) *"One cannot read without indignation such things written in a lordly, scornful tone about an old worker. I think the tone of such talk is absolutely impermissible for a Soviet writer."*

How should we respond to criticism such as this? It would be patronizing of us to support Nekrasov either with righteous anger or righteous sympathy. We can only remember what he learned from the antagonists he met in Italy that "humor is the best weapon against hostile people."

And if we read *Both Sides of the Ocean* as the testimony of a renegade Communist, as a dissonant voice in the chorus of our opposition, wouldn't we be just as dogmatic as the Stalinists we number among Nekrasov's enemies? Nekrasov brings his intelligence and sensitivity to Italy and America, but he brings his Communist ideas as well. Standing before the Lincoln Memorial, he asks himself:

> *Could Abraham Lincoln have foreseen, could this fighter for truth and justice have imagined what would happen in only half a century, that some of his descendants, the descendants of Washington and Jefferson, would try to smother the young Soviet Republic just born on the other side of the world?*

He refers of course to the Allied intervention in Russia during and after World War I. His question assumes the justice of Communist teaching, that the intervention was the attempt of the forces of reaction to destroy a democratic regime, not as we know it, in part at least, as a desperate and confused Allied effort to raise the Russian armies again on the eastern flank of Imperial Germany. The question occurs to him as he stands before the monument to Lincoln. By the artist's act of imagination, he projects it into the figure sitting before him, "in the shadowy light of the chilly marble hall." But in itself, the question is not very different from what we find in the ideologist's handbook, except in one respect: Nekrasov doesn't know the answer.

Nekrasov wrote this book with humor, compassion, and wonder. He wrote it because in his own words, it makes him ashamed to see people take pleasure in the misfortunes of others. We can only read him the way he writes. The significance of his book is not only that it has been attacked by the Soviet government. If we thought so, how much better would we be than the Soviet journalist who wanted to see the slums?

For there is only one enemy in *Both Sides of the Ocean*. The enemy is not Stalinism, or dogmatism, or even communism, though communism may be irretrievably imbued with it. The enemy is banality. Nekrasov attacks this enemy on every page. With every paragraph that begins, "Here I anticipate what my future critics will say . . ." he predicts the line his critics will take before they have opened his book. And how ironic it must have been for him to see them popping up with cries of shame exactly as he knew they would, Khrushchev among them, puppetlike at his conjuror's bidding. For who could resist the humor of Nekrasov's treatment of the old gray worker, except the hackneyed old Worker himself?

Nekrasov quotes the Russian saying, "Dead water can only stick the broken body together, but living water pours life into the soul." *Both Sides of the Ocean* is a complaint against dead water. It is a plea for a fair and humane view of the world, for what is humorous and lyrical in a world crowded by ideology. It is a plea for monuments to the past that are vanishing now in a landscape of mass construction. It is a plea for books and movies that are not read or shown, for paintings that are not seen. *Both Sides of the Ocean* is a plea for the barriers of the mind to be taken down so that the world can flow into it. It is living water.

Elias Kulukundis

New York
November 1963

ITALY

So you went to Italy again?"

"Yes."

"How did you like it?"

"Well . . . I got terribly tired. . . . Anyway, two weeks is such a short time. . . ."

"Yes, that's true. . . . But still . . ."

"Well, how can I tell you . . . ? Naturally I found it interesting."

"What do you mean naturally you found it interesting?"

"Well . . . for the usual reasons. We did so much running around in those two weeks—actually, to be exact, we had thirteen days—there was so much to talk to people about, so much to see, that it will take me about six months to figure it all out."

"Mm. Yes . . . of course."

He was silent after that. I could see his dissatisfaction in the way he looked at me. It was the same look that I must have given, ten years earlier, to one of our famous writers who was always sent to any kind of congress. As he hung up the telephone, I heard him snarling: "Now I'm in for it! I have to go to Paris again."

He saw how surprised I was and he explained it to me: "If you only knew how tiresome I find all these trips—Paris, Stockholm, Geneva. You run around like a squirrel on a treadmill. You can't do any work, and you don't get any rest either."

I was surprised and indignant, even personally offended.

And now I felt this man looking at me in the same way: "The poor thing got so tired, you see. Two weeks was just not long enough for him. He had too many impressions, he saw too much, and now he just can't digest it all."

I felt him thinking all this and I felt uncomfortable.

I first went to Italy five years ago. I stayed there about a month. I tried to put down my impressions in an essay called "First Acquaintance." As I was writing it, I kept telling myself: "These are all only my first impressions, after all. Maybe someday I'll go to Italy a second time. Then I can try to deepen my acquaintance, widen it, cultivate it." And then that "second time" came about. It came about in March, 1962. Did it turn out the way I planned? The way I hoped it would? No, it didn't. Anyway . . .

Question: What's the best way to get to know a country when you're only going to be there a short time?

There are many answers. Probably this is the best one:

You're planning to go to Italy, you say. Then be so good as to go to the library, dig around in the specialized literature, read up on whatever interests you most. That way, by the time you get to Italy, you won't have to ask questions which you could have answered at home. That's the first step. That's your groundwork. Second, make up a list of people and places you want to see, even if it's only approximate, and try your best to keep to it. Third, don't waste your energy; don't try to see everything, concentrate on what you really want to see. Fourth, don't ever let go of

4

your notebook; don't ever rely on your memory. Fifth, don't go to bed late, but get up early; there's nothing more beautiful than the morning, either at home or abroad. Sixth, stay in one place for a while; it's better than hopping all over Europe. And, finally, seventh, learn the language. If you don't, you won't be worth two cents.

Those are the seven commandments. Keep them and they'll serve you in good stead. Break them and you'll have only yourself to blame.

My God, how I told myself I had to keep the commandments. I pleaded and pleaded with myself, but it was no use. I did stay in one place for a while, and I did do some reading, but except for these two, I didn't keep them. And strange as it may seem, I'm not even sorry. I'm only ashamed I didn't keep the seventh one: I didn't learn the language.

But it's not a matter of having a plan of action, an itinerary or a notebook. What usually turns out to be much more interesting is just the opposite: the unexpected, a chance meeting, a new acquaintance, a sudden argument, a question that takes you by surprise. In other words, I was interested in upsetting schedules, my own and other people's. I'll have a lot to say later about these little violations. They don't have as much to do with our trip to Italy as they do with our trip to America, and with the general organization of the Soviet tourist industry. But right now, let me say a few words about notebooks, about the writer's notebook.

It was on my first trip to Italy that I first saw the crowds of tourists in the Vatican, mostly West Germans, filling page after page of their notebooks. They wrote down everything the guides told them, even though most of it was already written down in the guidebook each one of them kept tucked under his arm. It was then that I began to dislike the notebook. And I liked it even less when I got to America and saw some of our tourists doing the same thing: writing incessantly, unable to spare so much as a glance at the paintings that hung in front of them. By Antwerp, I had come to hate it. As we walked past one of the ancient buildings, our guide happened to mention that it was the palace where King Baudouin stays whenever he comes to Antwerp.

"Which one? Which one?" Someone was pulling at my sleeve, one of the more alert of the young women in our group.

"That one," I told her.

I couldn't resist looking over her shoulder as she started taking it down: *The palace where King Baudouin stays whenever he comes to Antwerp.* And the next moment, afraid to miss the next palace coming up, she trotted after the guide.

You will say that no one forces you to write down all kinds of useless information. It all depends on the person taking the notes. That may be true, but in my opinion, a writer needs a notebook only for addresses and phone numbers. For anything else, it just gets in the way.

The very magic of writing, its selectivity, if we can put it that way, later destroys the spontaneity of remembrance. In a way, the same thing happens to you as when you tell a story again and again. Soon you are only "making small talk." Your story has turned into a polished performance. And all its details, each one tested by rehearsal, become rooted in place, yielding no room to any others.

I don't know about other people, but I'm against the notebook.

My hatred was made complete about a year and a half ago in my native Kiev, when Danilo Dolci came to visit us.

He is a great Italian public figure, the holder of a Lenin Prize. In the past he was an architect in Trieste, but now he has settled permanently in Sicily in order to live among peasants and fishermen and devote his whole life to them. He is a kind, honest, selfless person: his life can be admired and emulated. Money means nothing to him: he is almost a beggar himself. Anything he does have, he gives to the peasants and fishermen, trying to give them a bearable existence. I met him in Italy in 1957. He very much wanted me to visit him in Sicily, but as usual, itineraries and time-tables got in the way, and I never made it. Then he came to the Soviet Union to get to know our planning system: maybe he will be able to adapt some of it for his own country.

In Kiev he was busy all day, running around from ministry to planning office to economic council. I dropped in on him at his hotel for an hour or so, just to say hello and have lunch with him. But we had barely sat down at the table when he pulled out his notebook. He wrote down every word I said; he didn't miss a thing. Maybe he had to do that. Maybe it was important for him to write it down. But I was sorry just the same. I came to have a chat with him, and instead I had an interview.

Yes, I'm definitely against notebooks, against inspection tours and planned visits, and I'm against timetables. The most interesting things come up suddenly, against every expectation. It's better that way, even if the unexpected has its disadvantages, its reefs and rapids.

For a beginning, let me tell about something that happened, not in Italy, but in the Soviet Union. But it happened to an Italian. And it still gives me the shivers to think about it.

The Italian was Giulio Einaudi, the great publisher from

7

Turin, the son of a former president, and a friend of the Soviet Union who has done a great deal to make Soviet literature popular in Italy. He came to the Soviet Union with his wife and a friend, the Venetian writer Carantoto-Gambini.

They spent two or three days in Kiev, driving around the city and taking in all the sights. But then suddenly Einaudi wanted to go to see a market place. Foreigners are generally interested in market places for some reason, but in addition, somebody had told Einaudi that the market was the only place where you could get real pieces of folk art. As we found out later, the folk art he was talking about was nothing more genuine than swans painted on oilcloth and papier-maché cats with huge lobster eyes. But if Einaudi wanted the market place, then the market place it was. We got into the Intourist car and went to the Zhitny Market in the Podol quarter. An interpreter and a friend of mine came along with us. We got there without any trouble at all. As we got out of the car, Einaudi asked if he could take pictures in our country.

"Of course," I said. "Everything except strategic and military installations."

The next moment Einaudi was surrounded by people. And they were far from silent. They were accusing him of taking a picture of an old woman selling ants (probably as a cure for rheumatism). Some of them even maintained that the picture was taken for espionage purposes. Anyway, one way or another, the defendant and his accomplices, we three Soviet citizens, found ourselves in the local police station. And as police stations go, I might add, this one was hardly a showcase. They kept us there forty minutes. They made phone calls, interrogated us, they demanded that we turn over the film. And it was only after we did some very fast talking ("He is the son of a president. He is the director of a great publishing house!") that they apologized and let us go. Even then it was not before they made some final phone calls. I must say that during those forty minutes, which we spent in the company of drunks from the market place sleeping in the corner, our famous publisher bore himself with great dignity. He even tried to console me.

"These things happen," he kept telling me in Russian. "They happen sometimes."

Afterward in Moscow, they say he made the incident into a very amusing anecdote. In Italy, he said, an affair like this would have lasted several hours at least. And in general, he was very happy with his trip. The only thing he was sorry about was that he never did get his folk art. No marketwoman would agree to sell him any. One of them told me the reason.

"If I had known who it was for," she said, "I would have made something artistic. But this . . ."

Tell me, what did you find most interesting in Italy or America?"

The first few times someone asked me this, I couldn't give a straight answer. Now I can. What I found most interesting was the arguments. I won't say they were the easiest part of the trip, but they were the most absorbing. And perhaps they were an essential part of it. But more of that later. For now, let me just say that I enjoyed them the most.

I often wonder what gives you the most satisfaction: when the people around you know who you are, or when they don't?

I don't want to be coy. It's very flattering to take a place at a "round table" (an oval one, in fact) in the Marinoli Palace with Alberto Moravia, Carlo Levi, Pier-Paolo Pasolini, Guido Piovene and Soviet writers representing our literature in Rome. And appearing on television in Rome is also fun. Just imagine it, you and the director of *Ballad of a Soldier,* you and Grigori Chukhrai, are the first Soviet people to be in that enormous, heavily guarded building, run by people who are far from sympathetic to our system and our point of view. Chukhrai is absolutely calm (he's so used to it, damn him!), but I'm nervous. I'm almost as nervous as the pretty young interpreter whose whole career and future depend on how she handles the speeches of these two *sovieticos*. And her husband is there sitting next to her, newly wed, worried for his bride. But you can rest assured now. It came off perfectly. And the next day the young couple sent touching little souvenirs to Chukhrai and me, and bags of sugared almonds, the traditional gift of newlyweds.

Why hide it? It makes you feel good to be popular.

But all the same, it's not the most enjoyable thing.

I don't know about others, but when I see a good film (like *The Engineer* with Pietro Germi or *Prairie Street* with Jean Gabin), I can't help imagining myself sitting at a table in one of those Paris bistros where Gabin and his friends argue about the bicycle races; or taking a seat, with my glass of Chianti, next to Germi the engineer as he sits there a little bit drunk and feeling gloomy. How we came to love this big, gray drinker, hard and softhearted at the same time. And how we loved his wife, who has to think for everyone and make all the decisions and be responsible for everything. And the children, especially the youngest one, a charming little rascal with black eyes. And how we loved the café where the engineer always stopped in after work, even on New Year's Eve. And the bartender, too.

And now you are in that country itself. In the engineer's country, in his home town.

In one day we flew across almost all of Europe. Half an hour to Warsaw, three hours to Paris.* Then across the peak of the Mont Blanc rising through the storm clouds and on to Rome. The Fuimichino Airport glittering with

* There is no direct flight from Moscow to Rome. (*Translator's note*)

light and glass (I can't decide which is better, the new Orly in Paris or Fuimichino). Then a bus past the Coliseum to Termini Station, Rome's train station. Ten o'clock at night. Ahead of us, a four-hour train ride to Florence, to our ultimate destination.

We got into the car, rammed our suitcases onto the luggage racks. We were moving. I opened the window and leaned out. I leaned out and found myself in a movie called *The Engineer*. By heaven, it was the same railroad station, the same train, the same wheels clattering faster and faster over the switches and crossings, the little huts flashing by, the poles, the houses. . . . But who was driving the train? When we got to Florence—she greeted us with rain, cold, and damp—I couldn't help it, I looked in the window of the locomotive. You may laugh at me if you like. It was Pietro Germi. I swear it was!

I couldn't find the café where the engineer played the guitar and sang songs with his friends. Actually, I didn't look for it. But I was in another café, one that he might have gone to. And Cabiria might have been there, too. And any character out of *Rome—11 O'clock*. They were playing some kind of game there. I got myself some beer and started playing, too. It was a game run by electricity, with a movable arm that sweeps over a large board spread with all kinds of tempting items: brooches, cases, cigarette holders. You put fifty lire into the slot and press a button. Then the arm begins to move. When it gets right over the thing you want, you press another button and the arm stops and a scoop drops down and either catches your prize or misses it. I missed it every time. I spent about three hundred lire, and I gave fifty more to a red-haired, freckled *paisano,* but neither of us got anything back for it. No one else did either, except for a fellow in overalls who looked like a taxi driver: he came off with a penknife. But everyone had a good time. There was loud laughter, especially if someone came very close to his prize and missed it. And they were all drinking beer. They would dig deep in their pockets and put more money in the slot. After a while some wives would try to take their husbands home. But they refused. They drank more beer. They were all having a good time. And so was I. I felt at home in this worker's café on the outskirts of town. No one was paying any attention to me. Or rather, they were paying just as much attention to me as they were to anyone else. And that's what's really enjoyable.

There were other times like that. We were wandering around Florence late at night, a couple of friends and I. It was very late. The streets were empty. We were walking nowhere in particular, wherever our eyes were taking us, up and down the streets and alleys, along the banks of the Arno. Then we came to the Ponte Vecchio. It's an ancient bridge, hundreds of years old. It is the most picturesque bridge in the world, a bridge and a street at the same time. It has shops of all sizes on it, mostly jewelry shops. There must be a million pictures and post cards of it, pictures taken in all shades of daylight and from every angle. I took pictures of it, too, but I've been sketching it ever since I was a child. A famous bridge. It was a miracle it survived the war, even though the battle front passed right through Florence and up the Arno.

And now we were standing on that very bridge, our elbows on the railing. We gazed down at the Arno racing beneath us, with the lights of nocturnal Florence reflected in it. Then suddenly two night watchmen came toward us. They wanted to know if we could give them a smoke. One of us spoke Italian and we had a talk. And in a few minutes do you know what we were talking about? About Chile.

About who was going to win the international soccer championships.

Talking about soccer on the Ponte Vecchio? You think that's blasphemy? I don't. In those five or six days we had spent in Florence, the Ponte Vecchio had turned gradually from an acquaintance into a friend, and we were not exactly tourists any longer.

Five years ago, when I came to Piazza della Signoria for the first time, I went into the Palazzo Vecchio almost on tiptoe. I had butterflies as I went into the famous courtyard, up the stairway and into the enormous hall decorated with Vasari paintings and sculpture by Michelangelo. It was holy ground.

But this time, the Palazzo Vecchio was not only a famous monument to a style of architecture and an era. It was also the place where we sat with our earphones on, listening to the speeches of the delegates to the congress of the European Society of Writers. We held our meetings in the Hall of the Five Hundred (the one with the Vasaris and Michelangelos). During the official receptions there were guards at the entrances and on the stairways, dressed in medieval clothing, bearing torches and halberds. And as you might expect, toward the end of the congress, everyone was a little tired. Is it any wonder that some of us couldn't last until the end of the last few meetings and slipped off into the city to wander around the quiet streets? The Palazzo Vecchio didn't hold it against us. It was a friend of ours, too, and in a true friendship, etiquette only gets in the way.

But my friend from Kiev, the architect, held it against us. I was telling him about something or other, and I happened to let slip that one evening I just didn't feel like going to the Palazzo Vecchio. I'd been there every day, you see, morning and evening.

"Well, what are we coming to?" he said, and there wasn't a trace of sympathy in his voice. "And, for that matter, didn't you get bored with Florence itself? Morning and evening, night and day?"

I began to feel uncomfortable.

Yes, what's most enjoyable is when you stop thinking of yourself as a tourist. When you begin to feel a little bit at home. When you walk home from the Villa Borghese to the Impero Hotel near the Termini Station and you don't have to ask anyone how to get there. When you don't gape at the station any more, but think of it only as the place where you can pick up a *Paris-Match* with the latest install-ment of "Reminiscences of Hemingway" by his younger brother. When you can say to your friend, the soccer fan, "By the way, tomorrow there's a good game at Flaminio Stadium, Rome *vs.* Milan. Are you interested? It isn't far. Near the station you take a Number Sixty-nine bus to Flaminio Square and you're right there. You can take a Number Thirty-three if you want to, but that way you have to change." (Yesterday I walked all over that stadium be-cause it was built by Pier-Luigi Nervi, the famous Italian architect, but today I talk about it as though it were our own Dynamo Stadium.)

There is another thing that gives an indescribable pleas-ure: the second meeting. The meeting which shows you something new and unexpected in what you thought you already knew.

I don't overdo museums. I prefer to see a little, but see it thoroughly. In the Uffizi in Florence, I walked through ten rooms, no more. I rediscovered Bronzino, Filippino Lippi, Paolo Ucello. Especially Ucello. Actually, I must admit something, even if I'm ashamed of it: I hadn't known a thing about him; I was seeing him for the first time.

As I went into one of the first rooms of the Quatrocento, a painting struck me suddenly and unexpectedly, and I stopped to look at it. How could I have missed it when I was here before? That's what I mean by the tourist rush. It was an extraordinary painting. It was called "The Battle." I don't know anything that compares with it for delicacy and rhythmic perfection of composition, for precision of design, the striking audacity in the way the different colors are combined, and finally, for the perfect way that the foreground and background are both joined together and separated at the same time.

The first thing you see when you come into this room is a horse kicking up its hind legs in the right-hand side of the picture. There are two more horses, fallen horses, sky blue. Why are they sky blue? I don't know. But they have to be. And you can't take your eyes off the painting. In the foreground, knights are joined in battle. In the middle, on a white mount, a soldier is struck down by the thrust of a spear. The spear is unbelievably long, cutting through the picture in a powerful horizontal. To the left and right, there is a forest of spears, creating a rare beauty, an almost musical rhythm. All this is against a background of fields, crisscrossed by little planted strips, and tiny foxhounds jumping among them. Farther on, beyond the hills, more battalions are marching.

Have I described the painting? Really, you hardly can. I seem to have trouble describing what is striking about it. It's a magic combination—I can't find a better adjective— of the symbolic and the real. The flat, two-dimensional quality of the painting is never broken. There is no illusion in it, but it does have depth, a depth that is created not by the elementary principles of perspective (by the way, Ucello was a great master of them), but by something else, something much closer to art. The flatness is never broken, but kept perfectly consistent throughout the painting. For that reason, the sky is not shown, since that would immediately have created the *illusion* of depth. No, there is no illusion. The depth is created only by the planes, by the size of the figures in foreground and background. Not to describe, but to express: that is the essence of Ucello. . . . And now I know why those fallen horses are sky blue. They are dead. It is an expression of death. And at first I thought the painter needed these two sky-blue patches in the foreground for a balance of colors, like the hares and foxhounds in the background.

Who was this wizard of the early Rennaissance, Paolo di Dono, called Ucello? (It means the bird. They say he was very fond of animals, especially birds.) He was a Florentine, the son of a barber. He was a jeweler, a mosaic maker. He designed the stained-glass windows for the famous Florentine cathedral. He worked with Ghiberti and was a friend of Donatello. He lived a great life, and died in 1475. Most of his works have not survived. The most outstanding one, "The Battle," was underestimated by his contemporaries, and indeed by us, too.

Here's what Giorgio Vasari writes about him in his famous *Biographies of the Most Famous Painters, Sculptors and Architects:*

> *Paolo Ucello would have been the most refined and inventive genius since Giotto if he had only treated the human and animal figure with half the time and enthusiasm which he spent on problems of perspective. . . . Paolo Ucello was by nature a man of subtle and flexible intellect, but he found no other satisfaction than trying to solve difficult or impossible problems*

of perspective. . . . Paolo worked without rest in an eternal pursuit of the most difficult artistic problems. Finally, he gained so much experience in these problems that he found the manner, the methods, and the fixed principles for showing upright figures in such a perspective that, one after another, they would grow shorter and accordingly smaller until finally they would disappear altogether. . . . Until then this had only been done by accident. . . . All these inventions made him keen on solitude almost to the point of misanthropy, and for weeks and sometimes months he would stay at home without so much as exchanging a word or two with anyone and without receiving visitors. He spent all his time on these conundrums, and at the end of his life he found himself a pauper instead of a famous man. Thus he lived to a very old age, reaping little gladness from it, and finally he died in the eighty-third year of his life. He was survived by his wife and daughter. His wife used to recall how he would spend all night in his studio in pursuit of the principles of perspective, and when she would call him to bed, he would only exclaim, "Ah, this wonderful perspective!"

It seems to me that Vasari is unfair to Ucello. All you have to do is look at "The Battle" in the Uffizi (only the center of the triptych is there; the left side is in London, the right in the Louvre) to realize that Paolo di Dono, nicknamed Ucello, deserves his fame not on account of perspective alone. Anyway, what can you say of a period which produced Cimabue, Giotto, Ucello, Ghiberti, Massacio, Brunelleschi, Donatello, Piero della Francesca and a dozen more, one right after the other? What can you say of a period which gave the world Michelangelo?

Confronting Michelangelo is a joyous experience. Once again, I paid homage to Moses and to the Pieta in St. Peter's. But there were too many people there, and they were putting up some kind of partitions, in preparation for the holiday. In St. Peter in Chains there were booths with earphones next to Moses: you drop your money in and a recording tells you all about it in Italian, French, English, or German. A group of American sailors was crowding around the English booth. I dropped my money into the French one, and put the earphones on, but right away the whole thing made me want to be outside again.

On the other hand, in San Lorenzo, there was no one in the Chapel of the Medici.

The Chapel of the Medici.

I always thought it was an exaggeration when people said you can stand for hours in front of the Sistine Madonna. Now I don't think so. I stood there no less than an hour. For me, the Chapel of the Medici is unquestionably the greatest work of art. The world knows no more perfect synthesis of sculpture and architecture. The force of its emotion is tremendous. What's the secret? That's the riddle.

When you look at the epitaph of Lorenzo and Juliano di Medici, everything looks perfect to you: the depth of the conception, the way it is expressed, the plasticity of the figures themselves. No, I'm not using the right words. Before you is something beautiful. That's all. There is nothing to add to it, and nothing to take away. The utmost perfection.

Perfection. Then why are the faces on the figures unfinished, the ones that represent Morning and Evening? * It's hard to imagine that Michelangelo simply wasn't able

* Obviously, the Russian gives us an incorrect translation here. In Italian it's not Evening but "Twilight" [*il Crepuscolo*], not Morning but "Dawn" [*l'Aurora*], which is more precise. [*Author's footnote.*]

to finish them; even then Vasari used to finish Michelangelo's works for him. And a great genius would hardly have found time for insignificant details (such as the capitals of the columns, with their tiny masks of smiling creatures with sheep's horns) without finishing what was essential.

In his excellent book *Images of Italy,* P. Muratov writes:

> *The liberation of the spirit, creating form out of inert and formless matter, has always been the great purpose of sculpture. Sculpture became the dominant art form of antiquity because the world view of the ancients presupposed the divinity of all matter. . . . But the world for Michelangelo was no longer the native abode of the spirit which it had been for Greek sculptors, or its beautiful new domain, which it had been for the painters of the early Rennaissance. In his sonnets, he writes of immortal forms doomed to enclosure in an earthly prison. His chisel liberates the spirit, not for a harmonious coexistence with matter such as the ancients had conceived, but rather to separate the two. But the unworkable pieces of stone, intruding as they do on the perfection of the spiritual form, are only proof of the impossibility of this separation, of the ultimate strength of the earthly bonds.*

Was Muratov right? Is that what Michelangelo had in mind when he created these enigmatic figures? Or does the explanation better apply to those captive figures just now struggling with their marble bonds at the Academy of the Arts? I don't know. This is a mystery to me, and I cannot solve it.

All these questions occurred to me on my second trip to San Lorenzo. The chapel is empty. There is silence all around. In the distance, the sound of bells, not our kind, not Russian bells. It adds something, like the organ of a Gothic cathedral. I am sitting in a great leather armchair. I feel that I am dissolving into everything around me. But not my brain: my cursed brain won't be quiet. It keeps asking questions. Why? Why? What is the meaning of the unfinished hand of "Night" resting on the mask of sleep? Is it an accident? And the little mask of the man with a mustache on the back of Giuliano de Medici, which they noticed only when they took the figure off its pedestal for restoration. It is all a mystery.

The madonna and child is another mystery. Why is the left hand of the infant Christ unfinished? Why is it obviously incorrect anatomically? And finally, why is all the sculpture, standing against the background of the smooth white walls, separated from the architecture of the chapel, obviously by intention, when the chapel itself is a synthesis of sculpture and architecture?

No, we still haven't solved these mysteries, even in our era of the split atom and the spaceship. We have not penetrated art's mystery of mysteries. Venus di Milo is beautiful even without arms. They say there are people looking for them now, somewhere on the bottom of the Aegean Sea. But what will that solve?

Twenty pages have gone by already. A fussy reader will be full of righteous indignation. What a confusion! The author goes from one thing to another. It's too bad he broke his second commandment. A plan would have made this smoother, easier to follow.

Well, I have nothing to give this reader to cheer him up. What follows is only more of the same. Of course, I could have done it like an encyclopedia:

Italy
1) *Geographical location*
2) *Population*
3) *System of government*
4) *History*
5) *Industry*
6) *Agriculture*
7) *Art, etc.*

But I didn't want to. Too boring. And telling everything in order is boring, too. I remember when a friend of mine came back from a trip and started telling us about it. He pulled out his notebook (again the infernal notebook) and started off:

"So, on the first day, we arrived at such and such a place, on the second at such and such, on the third——"

Here someone interrupted him to ask a question.

"Oh, that happened on the sixth day. I haven't come to that yet."

But he never did come to that: we were sitting around a large dinner table, and there were many other people there.

Anyway, let me say that I promise no order whatsoever. But just so I don't offend the pedantic reader, the devotee of absolute clarity, let me make a little report.

On March 11, 1962, the Soviet delegation flew to the congress of the European Society of Writers in Florence, Italy. The Soviet delegates included: A. Surkov (Chairman), M. Bazhan, V. Panova, A. Tvardovsky, G. Chukhrai, and G. Breytburd (Secretary). Among those invited to attend the congress as guests were: I. Andronikov, S. Antonov, E. Vinokurov, A. Voznesensky, D. Granin, E. Kazakevich, V. Nekrasov, I. Ogorodnikova, N. Tomashevsky, V. Shklovsky. Delegates and guests took part in meetings of the assembly and the congress of the Society in Florence from March 11 to March 15, and a "round table" discussion in Rome on March 16. In addition, they met with members of the Italy-USSR Society, with individual writers, painters, film directors, and students of the University of Rome. They also appeared on television. In addition to Rome and Florence, the group visited the following cities: Prato, Ravenna, Siena, and San Gimignano. On March 24, the Soviet writers returned home by air.

In addition to the foregoing, let me say: Beside conferences and round-table discussions, there were also receptions, luncheons, and dinners, which in all cases proved impossible to avoid, despite the fact that they are not the ideal means of getting to know a country. For example, we spent no more than three hours in San Gimignano, one of the most beautiful cities in Italy, and for two out of these three hours we were seated at table (in a very colorful restaurant to be sure), appeasing our hunger and proposing toasts. Let me conclude these remarks by saying that on that very morning we had already had two "minor receptions" in Siena, one at the mayor's house and one at the city hall, and in the evening we addressed the members of Italy-USSR Society on the subject of the Soviet film.

We didn't want to leave Florence. She is not a big city, and we had grown used to her so quickly, reached an intimacy with her. We strolled along her parks and streets, we went to the museum, and we found the house where Dostoevsky lived when he was writing *The Idiot*. We wanted to find the exact apartment, but nobody could tell us which it was. A young man came down the staircase—a very Dostoevskian staircase—and informed us that Signor Dostoevsky didn't live there any more. Actually, he said, he died a long time ago.

We met interesting people, nice people. We drank Chianti with them, and not only Chianti for that matter. We bought souvenirs and post cards, we exchanged matchboxes and postage stamps, and as we were leaving, La Pira, the mayor of Florence, or the *sindaco* as the Italians call him, gave us souvenir medallions of the congress with their graceful Florentine lilies.

No, we didn't want to leave. Florence seemed the most beautiful city in the world, with its Duomo, its Signora, and the David, the turbid yellow Arno with its bridges arching over it; the bystreets; the grayish-brown tiling of the roofs; the wistful ring of the bells of Santa Croce waking us up in the morning. We thought we would never see anything as beautiful as that. We parted sadly.

And then we came to Siena.

Siena is almost as well known as Florence. At one time the two cities quarreled. They were rivals in both politics and art. And both of them have given great painters to the world. Siena's fame began in the twelfth century. She is called the city of the Italian gothic: the Sienese cathedral is one of its rare examples. Siena is the birthplace of the Sienese school. Siena is the heart of Tuscany, the center of the wine industry, the mother of Chianti. Travertine, the Sienese marble, is known throughout the world. And in addition, Siena is strikingly beautiful, perched on the crest of her hills.

I was a little uneasy as we drove into the city. There were so many new apartment houses, so many cubic buildings. But by the time we got to the center of town, my worries were over. Even Florence faded a little in comparison. It was all the middle ages. There were bystreets clinging to the hillsides, staircases, arcades, little squares suddenly emerging, courtyards with fountains in them. And it was all out of the fourteenth century, the thirteenth, the twelfth. And it was all in that special shade of reddish brown, the Sienese color, the color of the Tuscan landscape.

The Tuscan landscape. I have seen many beautiful roads in the world: the Georgian-Military road to Lake Ritsa, the serpentine windings in the Crimea, the roads of Saxony, of Schwartzwald, of Southern Bohemia, and Slovakia. But none of them can compare with the road from Siena to San Gimignano.

A sunny spring day, wondrously clear. The road weaves in and out among the hills, through patches of forest, through silvery olive groves. Now it breaks free into a valley, and before you the line of the horizon opens out with such beauty and such delicacy that you hold your breath. I have never seen such a horizon anywhere. It is amazingly clear. Hilly and winding. The trees seem painted on it with a tiny brush, and so do the castles on the crests of the hills, and the belfries. . . . The reddish brown of the earth, the dull silver of the olive trees, the strident azure sky with tiny white tufts of clouds. Beautiful. And somehow familiar. Yes, of course, I've seen it all before. In the Uffizi. In the Palazzo Pitti. In Siena itself. "The Sienese School."

Suddenly there are towers on the horizon. Many, many towers. The road winds down through a vineyard. The towers disappear. Now they appear again. It is the town of the thirteen towers: San Gimignano.

What can you see after Florence and Siena? Anything? Well, you can see San Gimignano. And this one is really old. It is Dante. It is Boccaccio. It is the whistling of rapiers, the fluttering of capes, silk ladders hung down from balconies, the dying sound of lutes, the hollow steps of the night watch on the cobbled walks, the trembling flame of lanterns blown by the wind.

As you drive toward this town, you don't believe your eyes. Is it possible? Can such a thing exist in the middle of the twentieth century? Maybe it's only painted scenery? But who painted it? Who is the artist? The artist is the fourteenth century.

Similar towers, square and severe, once stood in Florence and Siena, too.* They were built by the noble fam-

---

* Looking at the towers of San Gimignano, I couldn't help thinking of the towers of Svanetia in Georgia. This little mountain country once lay on the route of the crusaders. Apparently, that is why the towers look alike. [*Author's note.*]

ilies. Little San Gimignano, situated between Florence and Siena, witnessed their rivalry. But only in this town, as though by a miracle, do the towers survive, still bearing the names of their former owners. There are Salbucci towers, Ardincelli towers. A miracle is a miracle, but besides that another reason San Gimignano looks the way it does today is that the town fathers as long ago as the seventeenth century declared every citizen personally responsible for the towers' preservation. Whoever permitted any destruction whatsoever was immediately responsible to restore it. *Per la grandezza della terra*—for the grandeur of the country. . . .

It was already evening. I was standing at a small lancet window of the Palazzo Comunale, looking down at the city. The sun was going down, and the towers, suddenly turned all red now, were throwing their whimsical shades back and forth. The sky was clear azure, just as before, with the white clouds. Between the towers you could see the Tuscan skyline and the tiled roofs, brown as the Tuscan soil. I stood by that window and thanked all those unknown town fathers of the seventeenth century for saving this beauty for me and for all of us, this fairy tale, this improbable beauty.

Per la grandezza della terra—for the grandeur of the country. . . . As we left San Gimignano behind us, and those towers which I may never see again, I could not help thinking of my native Kiev. As you come into it now, across the railroad bridge, you are suddenly thrilled by the cupolas of Lavra, shining anew in their restoration. You are glad to see the scaffolding around the Vydubetsky Monastery. And the Cathedral of St. Sophia seems younger now: the restorers have worked so long and carefully on her. But if you stand with your back to the cathedral and look across to the opposite side of the square, you see only impersonal roofs and fences. There, at one time, stood the monastery of Mikhail Zlatoverkhy. But now it is there no longer. It was torn down in 1937: torn down to make room for an office building which was never built. And now there is no more monastery of the eleventh century. Only those roofs and fences.

I would not recall this deplorable incident of twenty-five years ago if it did not seem to some people who are responsible for architectural monuments that every church or ikon is first of all "opium of the people" and only secondly a work of art. About a year or a year and a half ago I read an article in an influential Kiev newspaper which suggested that we should tear down certain eleventh- and twelfth-century churches and synagogues. They spoil the view, you see. A convincing argument, don't you think?

Not long ago I attended a conference in Kiev to review the list of monuments that are currently being preserved by the state. It is possible that all the buildings do not really qualify as monuments, and the state doesn't need to preserve all of them. But it is not only astonishing but alarming when a conference is called like that, "to review the list of monuments and cut it by fifty per-cent."

We love our history and our past, and we should carefully preserve what remains of our past, not destroy it.

Unfortunately, it is too late to talk about this now (at one time it was both talked and written about); it can only make you bitter to think of what is happening now on Mamayev Hill.* They are building something heavy and pretentious, covered with granite steps and bas-reliefs, and

* A hill near the present city of Volgagrad, of crucial importance in the Battle of Stalingrad. (*Translator's note*)

a thousand busts and statues. Of Mamayev's Hill as it was in 1942, when the whole world waited to see what would happen on its gentle slopes, of that Mamayev Hill, nothing will remain. Would it not have been better to keep it just the way it was in those days, with its trenches and shelters, its network of passages, and its bomb craters, the way it is dear to everyone, not only to those who fought there? It could have been reconstructed with absolute precision, down to the command posts of the platoons and companies, the disposition of the machine guns and forty-fives, the signs with the numbers of divisions, regiments, battalions, and companies.

Twenty years later (and after a hundred years it would have been even more interesting) the traveler could have walked right through the front lines on his way to the top of the hill, he could have climbed into a dugout, and seen the little stove itself that had been four steps away from death.* He could have touched a cannon, a machine gun, he could have looked through a telescope and calculated that the Germans had been a hundred meters, maybe sixty meters away. And that way I'm sure he would have learned far more about the Battle of Stalingrad than he will by standing on the granite steps of fancy staircases, at the foot of symbolic figures in bronze or gilded concrete that will soon be "decorating" Mamayev Hill.

When they were rebuilding Pavlov's house, someone had the idea to paint over all the inscriptions that people had scratched on the walls during the days of the siege. Before my very eyes, a reckless house painter with a thick brush

---

* A reference to the popular song, well known during the war, "Fire Flickers in the Little Stove." The lyrics include the following lines:

How far I must travel to be with you,
But I'm four steps away from my death.

(*Translator's note*)

plastered rosy paint over the historic (I'm not exaggerating) inscription, "This house was defended by Sergeant Yakov Pavlov and his men. . . ." Even then you couldn't read any more. It was impossible to stop the painter. And I barely had time to take a picture of that carving in its final moments. Now Pavlov's house stands smooth and pink and boring, as though it had never fought a battle.

In our regiment at Stalingrad, we often made fun of our first executive officer (he was a historian by profession) because he used to collect everything: plans, forms, summary reports, and despatches. "All this will be priceless someday," he said. And we would laugh at that: we thought it unworthy of a soldier to spend his time that way. But just a little while ago, I lost a shaving brush of mine, and I spent half a day in anguish until I found it. It was the only thing I still have that I had with me at Stalingrad.

Here I anticipate some of the remarks my future critics will make. So you went to Italy, they will say, and you saw a beautiful city, San Gimignano, which, thanks to some *sindacos* or other of the seventeenth century, has managed to preserve its ancient towers. And then through some kind of free association you started talking about Stalingrad. But in talking about it, for some reason you dwelt only on the omissions, on the oversights. And you didn't say a single word about the truly mighty work of reconstruction which embraced the entire city. And really, the city was built again completely new.

Yes, completely new. There has been a great deal written about that, a great deal. And it is an even greater pity that now there are some things which we cannot reconstruct any longer, even though at one time we had the chance.

But I mentioned Stalingrad not only because I was reminded of it by what I said about the preservation and reconstruction of the past, but for another reason, too. While I was in San Gimignano, I had an especially poignant realization of what Stalingrad means, not only to us Soviet people, but to everyone who hates fascism.

We were in that old restaurant with the heavy wooden beams and unplastered brick walls, the one which took up two of our three hours in San Gimignano. A young man at a neighboring table turned to address us. He was a member of the Christian Democratic Party. This is what he said:

"I am a Catholic, a convinced Catholic. I believe in God. But I want to say something to you people, you who come from a country of atheists. I want to say that we are thankful to you. You took your stand at Stalingrad. You fought there and died there not only for yourselves but for our sake, too, for people of different convictions, people from a different country, a country which at that time was fighting against you. At Stalingrad, you broke the back of fascism. And we thank you for that."

I cannot give you his exact words. But I have given you his thoughts exactly. They were thoughts spoken from an honest heart, and they found their way into my heart, into the heart of every one of us.

In Siena I met Carlo Montella, the writer. He lives in Pisa, but when he heard that we were going to be in Siena, he drove over in his car. I had met him the first time in 1959, in Yalta. He was at the writers' congress in Moscow and he came down for a few days with the well-known Haitian writer and public figure, Jacques Stephen Alexis, now imprisoned in his native land. Compared to Alexis, who is lively and sociable, Montella first struck me as gloomy and withdrawn. There were always people around Alexis; everything was always seething wherever he went.

But Montella would rather go for a walk by himself in the park. Then when I read his stories (several of them were published in our magazines), I realized that he is not gloomy at all. He is a man full of humor and irony, a truthful, candid person.

I rode in his car with him from Siena to San Gimignano. We didn't talk very much on the way, and there were three reasons for this: my poor knowledge of the French language, the amazing beauty of the landscape, and my concerted attempt to get all this beauty into my movie camera. Well, a little while ago, a friend of mine received a letter from Montella in which he wrote the following lines.

"I hope Nekrasov will excuse me for being so silent on our way from Siena to San Gimignano. I never talk when I drive anyway, but I wouldn't have talked much to him even if I hadn't been driving. I feel no need to talk to him because I realize he feels no need to talk to me. In this way we are alike, and we understand each other. But just the same I would like him to be my guest, and I would give him complete freedom. Tell him that."

The first few lines distressed me, but then the last ones reassured me somewhat. The need to talk? A difficult idea. Actually, the highest form of friendship is the freedom to be silent together. And I felt free to be silent with Montella. (Even though I can't exactly claim friendship with him yet.) Still, our conversation was not an indifferent one. On the contrary, it was interesting. Especially so because Montella is one of my most serious and demanding critics.

He didn't like *Kira Georgievna*. He didn't like *First Acquaintance* much either. He told me that straightaway. I should explain that when you're walking along the streets of Siena, it's very hard to listen to what anyone is saying, even if it's a criticism of your work. It's just not the place for talk. That may be why I didn't defend myself very force-fully. But a lot of what he said was true.

"You know," he said. "I didn't really believe the two anecdotes you included in *First Acquaintance,* the one about the lovesick *bersagliere* and the old gondolier with the frostbitten ears. You didn't make them up by any chance?"

I smiled without saying anything.

In general they were rather critical of *First Acquaintance* in Italy. They were friendly and encouraging, but critical just the same. The book came out there under the title *Sovietico in Italia,* which, of course, does not convey the apologetic tone of the Russian. It had a good press, some fifty articles or so. It was criticized—I know this from talk-ing to people; unfortunately, I couldn't read the articles —for a certain superficiality, for "touristic skimming."

"This is all very nice," they wrote. "It's interesting and smoothly written, but just the same, one could have asked for something deeper, . . . otherwise . . ."

One could have asked for something deeper? And how one could have asked! And how one goes on asking for that matter. For Italy is a country with an active, stormy, politi-cal life. Italy is a country of contrasts and contradictions, the country of the backward agricultural south and the flourishing industrial north, a country with a great cul-ture and a large percentage of illiterates, a country with the strongest Communist party in the bourgeois world and the tiny but powerful Vatican, a country of strikes and American missile bases, the country of *La Dolce Vita* and *Rocco and His Brothers.*

But to make any sense out of all this, to get that "some-thing deeper," you can't be a client of the Grandi-Viaggi Tourist Company. ("Grandi-Viaggi: The most beautiful and celebrated places in Italy in just two weeks!") You have to become such good friends with the Uffizi and the Vatican Museum that they won't be offended if you don't visit them. Instead of the Victoria Hotel on the Via Veneto or even the second-class Impero, you must stay with a simple working-class family, one like Germi the engineer's, even if his household is already complicated enough. And you have to stay longer than a week, longer than two weeks. . . . And most important, of course, you have to know the language. On that point, there is nothing I can say for myself.

I have something to say about other people, though, even if they are our friends. I don't think I met a single Italian without asking him to send me some information about the so-called "neocapitalism," especially about the Olivetti company which I described in my first book in the most general way. It is a very complex phenomenon, and you can't disregard it if you really want to understand contemporary Italy, especially the life of its working class. However many conversations I had with Italians, including Communists, I never got a clear, precise answer.

I said conversations, but, frankly speaking, where Italians are concerned, the word *conversations* is not very appropriate. Even if they don't begin as *arguments,* they end that way. And sometimes they end very heatedly, with raised voices and mutual recriminations.

And so I have arrived at what I said at the beginning, at what I thought was the most interesting part of my trip to Italy: the arguments, the discussions, those things which Italians hold especially dear and of which they are undisputed masters.

I had three kinds of discussions: (a) with unfriendly people whose purpose was to ask tricky questions and back us into a corner, (b) with people who were not of our camp, but who nevertheless were trying to find a common language, and finally (c) with our friends, mostly with Communists. Actually, these last were the hardest arguments of all.

On our last day in Rome, the poet Voznesensky and I were to speak before a meeting of the Italy-USSR Society. There were a lot of people there, and the room was small, hot and smoke-filled. It was hard to make speeches, especially after a strenuous day filled with all kinds of activities. But afterward there was a question period, and that's when things suddenly picked up and began to be fun. That was probably because the ones who took the most active part in the questioning were a correspondent for *Il Tempo* and an American student who had been a guide at the American Exhibit in Moscow. They both had only one thing in mind: to put us on the spot. The next day, in the airplane, we very much enjoyed the report of the evening in the government paper *Messagiero*.

"The Soviet writers amazed everyone," it said, "with the artistry, the humor, and the marksmanship of their answers, which were like rapier thrusts."

To this day, I can't understand why a newspaper by no means sympathetic to us decided to be flattering. It took no artistry to answer such questions as, "Is it true that, after one of Khrushchev's speeches, Yevtushenko was thrown out of the Komsomol?" Or, "Why don't you allow a single foreign book into the Soviet Union?" Maybe by artistry they meant how quickly we replied and not necessarily how intelligently. Anyway, humor is the best weapon against hostile people: Voznesensky and I tried not to forget it.

It was more difficult at the "round table" of the Palazzo Marinoli. The meeting was between Soviet and Italian writers and the discussion centered on the question of the commitment of contemporary writers. Our word *committed* has a different and somewhat cruder sound than the French *engagé*, but the meaning is clear. The question is whether or not a certain writer has joined a particular ideological camp. What ideas does he dramatize? What artistic course is he following? What forms does he use? The discussion aroused enormous interest. The hall was filled to capacity; even the aisles were full; and people were standing in the back rows, even standing on chairs.

Out in the street, at the entrance of the hall, some young people were passing out Fascist leaflets: "Moravia, Levi, Pasolini, don't meet with the Russians!" But the meeting did take place.

According to the Italian custom, there was no prearranged agenda. The presiding chairman Alatri (the general secretary of the Italy-USSR Society) called on people from the floor. And everyone could say whatever he wanted.

In my opinion, the discussion took on an unnecessarily academic character from the beginning, a theoretical and abstract character. I think it would have been more interesting and fruitful if the speakers had dealt in generalities a little less; if we had concentrated on some particular examples, actual books, films, and articles. I mentioned this in my own little speech: I said that I for one would have found it easier to speak if, for example, I had had a chance to see Pasolini's latest film, which was then being talked about all over Italy and all over Europe, too: *Accattone*. I didn't mean that I would have been able to express my complaints to the author, or on the other hand, my gratitude to him. (As a matter of fact, I did see the film after that and enjoyed it greatly, so I would certainly have done the second.) All I meant was that we Russians hardly know Italian criticism, just as Italians hardly know ours (to a

37

lesser extent). We don't know what we write about each other. That way we could have talked it all over and thrashed it out. And I think *Accattone* is just the kind of film to get people to lock horns over the general direction of the contemporary film, even the direction of art as a whole. In addition, if we could have brought along the newest Soviet film, *My Name Is Ivan,* by A. Tarkovsky— and if we had left ten days later, we could have taken it because it would have been ready—the discussion would have lasted two or three days at least.

It is very hard to have a discussion when everything between you, your opponent, and the audience has to pass through an interpreter, even if you have an excellent one, as we did. Pasolini mentioned this, in fact. He complained that Latin—the language of humanism, as he called it— had played a dirty trick on him twice in the discussion. But more of Pasolini later. Before him (he made two speeches), Piovene took the stand, and Moravia, Levi, Surkov, Panova, and Tvardovsky. (Tvardovsky also spoke a second time, in reference to Pasolini's second speech.)

And so the round-table discussion proceeded, on the question of the "Commitment of the Writer," the writer's duties. The Italians said a lot about the duties and obligations of our literature, but not very much about their own. Tvardovsky politely drew attention to some indelicacy in that approach.

"We are very grateful," he said, "that our Italian colleagues are so well informed on everything connected with our development. But personally, I would never have taken it upon myself to do the same for Italian art and literature."

"There's no comparison between us," they said. "Everyone is watching you, and so you are responsible." We heard that many times.

And that's how it went at the "round table."

The most interesting speech, in my opinion, was Pasolini's. He was more concrete than the others, and more trenchant.

Pier-Paolo Pasolini holds a foremost place in Italian literature. Unfortunately, we hardly know his novels and poems because he is very difficult to translate. His characters speak not only in dialect but in a lingo of the Roman suburbs that not even every native Roman can understand. *Accattone* is his first work for the screen; he wrote the scenario and directed it. It's an excellent film, and I'll have more to say about it later.

But what did Pasolini talk about?

He is a short man, with black hair and black eyes, and a simple, serious face that looks like a worker's or a peasant's. Until quite recently (he is thirty-five years old) he was a professional soccer player. Now he is a famous writer. He stood up and started to speak in a quiet voice. He told us he was dissatisfied with Soviet literature. In his opinion, Soviet literature is too naïve and sentimental. (Italians by nature are a very sentimental people, but they never allow any sentimentality in their art.) He singled out Aksenov's *Ticket to the Stars*, the poems of Yevtushenko, Chukhrai's *Ballad of a Soldier*.

"The builders of Soviet culture," he said, "are passing through a period of crisis, which we are following with great anxiety and sympathy. They are trying to overcome the inertia which is the legacy of the Stalinist period, and in order to do so they have decided, and rightly so, to bypass the period of decadence which we have had to experience. But in doing so, in leaping back across this experience of decadence, they have only encountered, to some extent, what came before it: romanticism, in the sense of innocence and purity. This romantic spirit, this sweet, good-natured spirit, full of gentle humor, and at its best, classically naïve and pure, cannot fully satisfy us now. The circumstances prevailing now in the Soviet Union and in our own country—because we are closely linked together—demand a treatment that is completely different. The Stalinist period was a real tragedy for all of us. In its turn, the technological progress that has followed it in Russia, and the awakening feeling of remarkable optimism, pose problems that are just as serious for all mankind. That rocket to the moon is not only a source of enormous pride for the Soviet Union. It forces us to consider from a fresh perspective—from every possible perspective, I might say—the suffering, the ignorance, and the poverty of the world itself. In this way, the circumstances are truly difficult. We expect the writers of the Soviet Union to create truly tragic works, bitter works, even brutal works if need be, in which all this may be expressed."

I have quoted such a long passage from Pasolini's speech because it was the only break in the academic tenor of the discussion, and it was the subject of most of the arguments we had. We did not agree that our art is naïve, or that it tries to avoid the tragic. (As evidence, we quoted Fadeyev's *The Rout,* Kazakevich's *The Star,* and Sholokhov's *The Silent Don.*) In his second speech, Pasolini tried to clarify his argument: that was where the Latin had played the trick on him. He had intended *naïve* in its strictly philological meaning, *ingenuo,* or *natural,* not naïve in the sense of innocent or childish. When he said that Chukhrai's art was naïve, he meant to pay Chukhrai a compliment.

There was also some confusion about the Italian *tragico.** What does Pasolini expect from our literature? Tragedy as a genre?

---

* In Russian there are two words for tragic: one pertains to tragedy as a genre, the other to tragedy in a more general sense, as a tragic accident. In Italian, as in English, there is only one word for both meanings.

At first glance, that seems to be what he wants. His talent is merciless. The philosophy of his work is the philosophy of hopelessness. But apparently that was not what he was asking of us (although, of course, he would like that, too). He explained that in his second speech, and he told us about the second trick his Latin had played on him.

"When I used the words *tragedy* and *tragic*," he said, "I didn't mean tragedy as a literary genre: the greatest tragedies are those that make us laugh. I was speaking about a tragedy that would fully satisfy our need to know everything about that historical and political tragedy of the recent past which Soviet writers have experienced so profoundly."

Tvardovsky * responded to Pasolini's request. He said that he always felt "awkward and a little afraid in that kind of discussion, when people try to deal with problems that would be difficult to solve even in solitude, when one probes his own mind in his moments of creation at the writing table."

That is true. There are some things that you must think over by yourself, before you can begin to write about them.

Dear Pasolini, after we had seen your film that night and you took us out to supper in the small restaurant, I am very sorry that you and I didn't tell each other what was uppermost in our minds. Maybe there were too many people there for such a serious dialogue. Or maybe we were too tired to argue any more. It would not have been an easy conversation, but I know it is a conversation that we shall have someday: we cannot help but have it. But before we do, I only want you and your friends to know one thing. (I hope they are our friends, too.) I want you to know that we remember those things you mean by tragedy; we remember them very, very well. But let me tell you, it is not

* Editor of *Novy Mir* and a poet in his own right, Tvardovsky is a leading Soviet theoretician on cultural affairs. (*Translator's note*)

so easy to talk about this, much less to write about it. Remember we are not talking about the tragedy of two or three people, or a hundred people or even a thousand. We are talking about the tragedy of an entire nation. And if our literature has not yet confronted all the complexity, the bitterness, and the contradiction of that period which we call "the cult of the individual," it is only a matter of time. It is impossible for Soviet literature to avoid those tragic events in our history, despite its impulse toward everything that is life-affirming (or perhaps on account of that impulse itself). It is impossible because, as Tvardovsky said at the end of his speech, "In art and literature, as in love, one may tell lies only for a time. Sooner or later the whole truth must be told." Dear Pasolini, I want you very much to understand this before we meet again, so that afterward —if we do meet—you won't say again as you said at the "round table," that you can talk to Russians, but you can't argue with them. Actually, it was probably because of the position you had taken that, sitting in the restaurant with you after seeing *Accattone,* we talked of anything at all, except the important thing.

On my first evening in Rome, right after the "round table," a group of journalists took me out with them.

"For the time being let's go over to the *trattoria*," they said, "Then later on we'll see."

At the *trattoria* they pushed a couple of tables together and brought out the decanters of Roman wine, both white and red: in Italy, no meeting can ever be held without them. (As a matter of fact, the Italians say that in Russia no meeting can be held without vodka, and that, they say, is a much more difficult proposition.)

I knew only two people in the company; the rest I was seeing for the first time. One was a certain Sergio, a young Communist, about thirty years old, a journalist, implacable and wicked. From that evening on until the day of my departure, I did nothing but fight with him.

Our acquaintance began with his telling me that he didn't like my speech at the "round table." Why not? Not bold enough. That was the first blow. Next he told me that he didn't like *Kira Georgievna*. Blow number two. And after that the blows came one after another. He was acute, obstinate, and needlessly bitter. He had shining black eyes that were sometimes gay and sometimes wicked, but mostly wicked. And I liked him very much. We fought over literature, art, journalism, different ways of life, social systems, methods of building communism, systems of elections, different trends in the movies. In other words, we fought over everything we talked about. Sometimes we reached such an intensity that we drove one of the girls in our group to tears.

"But why are you always fighting?" she sobbed. "Fighting! Fighting! Fighting! Can't you talk about something quiet for a change?"

Sergio and I drank a toast and tried to talk about something quiet, but in twenty minutes we were at it again. In other words, our conversation was conducted, as they say, in a spirit of party openness and frankness. And I liked that, I must say. I made friends with Sergio.

Italian Communists, the ones I've met anyway (both in Italy and in the Soviet Union), are not dogmatists and not revisionists. The decisions of the 20th and 22nd party congresses are just as important for them as they are for us.

For example, this is what they say:

"The decisions of these two congresses were absolutely correct. The cult of personality had to be exposed, and you did that with the courage that is characteristic of you. But you have to understand us, too. We live under different conditions. We live in the capitalist world, and it has laws of its own. You have only read about them in books—people in your generation, anyway—but we run up against them every day, every minute. Every Italian is constantly under the influence of two contradictory ideologies. And so the Italian—the worker, the employee, the peasant—has to choose between them. And in order to choose, he has to know which one is better. He reads the newspapers. He can buy any one he wants: the *Osservatore Romano* from the Vatican costs just as much as *Unita*. One paper says one thing, the other says the opposite. In one he reads that everything is bad in the Soviet Union; in the other that everything is good. Or at least up to a certain point that's what we used to write, that everything was good. Now it turns out that not everything is good by any means, not everything. . . . We used to write that Stalin was a great man, that he was infallible and wise. And they believed us, very many did. Now we write a lot more about his sins than we do about his infallibility, and they ask us what we were thinking of before.

"You have to understand that millions of people appeal to you now. For them you are the first nation in the world where the working class has come to power. And for that reason they want to know everything about you, everything as it is, both the good and the bad. That is what you don't always understand. We were all delighted at the success of Gagarin and Titov. But the ordinary Italian, especially one who has been to the Soviet Union (and there are more and more of these all the time), is bound to ask this question: 'How can it be that these people have sent a sputnik around the moon, and at home they still have to stand in line?' And he asks dozens of questions like it. They are not silly questions. They are essential. And we have to answer them. But it's up to you to answer. Too often you hesitate or evade the question, and while you're doing that, the answer is given for you—correct or incorrect—by the enemy. And people often listen to him. You don't take that into account."

That is what many Communists are saying now. And then they start in asking questions of their own. Why? Why?

A hundred thousand whys? Enough to start my head spinning.

And let me say this plainly, I found some of their questions very hard to answer.

Once I was talking to a young Italian film director, one who had been to the Moscow Festival last year. We were talking about *Naked Island,* the film that won the first prize, and he mentioned the names of two Japanese directors of whom I knew nothing: Mitsogushi and Kurosawa. He was surprised, but when he found out that I'd never seen anything by Bergman or Michelangelo Antonioni, he couldn't believe his ears.

"You've never seen anything by Antonioni?"

"No, I haven't?"

"But why not?"

I shrugged my shoulders. "We just haven't bought any of his films."

"You didn't buy any Antonioni's. He's the most famous director in the world. People argue about him everywhere. If you haven't seen his pictures, it's like saying you haven't seen *La Dolce Vita.*"

"But I haven't seen that either."

He threw up his hands.

"You haven't seen *La Dolce Vita?*"

"I haven't seen it."

"Well, you just don't like movies. You're obviously not interested in movies. I can't believe that you didn't buy *La Dolce Vita.* It's a very serious and intelligent film. It's a frightening film, a revealing film. I just can't believe it."

Another Italian asked me what I thought of Charlie Chaplin's last pictures, *Limelight* and *A King in New York.* Again I had to say that I hadn't seen them, that they weren't playing here.

46

"But why not? Chaplin is one of the great artists of our time. Every one of his pictures is an event."

I didn't know what to say. I myself don't know why his pictures aren't shown here. It's hard to believe the story that they're too expensive.

I was put on the spot for a third time by someone who asked me why we don't publish certain writers. (Here I remember how uncomfortable we felt, a group of us Soviet writers, including Panova and Granin, when six years ago in Leningrad, Alberto Moravia asked us what we thought of Kafka. We looked back and forth at each other and couldn't say a word: at that time we had never heard of him.)

"I understand that you have your own views of the role of literature," this person said to me. He was also a Communist, by the way. "I know you have your own publishing programs, and I'm willing to admit that some writers are closer to you and some are more distant. Some, I know, are completely alien. For example, if you suddenly decided to publish Nabokov's *Lolita,* the American 'best-seller,' it would simply be absurd. But why are you so slow with Faulkner? Why don't you publish Kafka? Why do you so studiously avoid Albert Camus? After all you don't have to publish them in editions of a hundred thousand copies. But every one of them is significant in his own way, even Sagan, who many people say is not a serious writer. These writers are extremely typical of their time, of an epoch, a frame of mind. You don't have to like them, you are free to criticize them, and you can finally reject them. But you must know them. . . ."

Was this person right? I think he was.

We do publish many translations of foreign literature now, from almost all languages of the world and in large editions. But all the same, there are many events in foreign literary life that pass us by completely. Or at best they reach us after a long delay.

By the way, the situation is much better now with translations of Soviet literature in Italy than it was three or four years ago, and much better than it is in any other Western country. For a while, Soviet books had only an exotic or sensational appeal, but that situation has changed radically in recent years. Now the number of writers they translate is much wider and more varied, not only prose writers but poets, too. With my own eyes, I saw editions in Italian book stores of works by Tendryakov, Kaverin, Vsevolod Ivanov, Ehrenburg, Kuznetsov, Aksenov, Berggolts, Aytmatov; plays by Arbuzov, Volodin, Khmelik, and Rozov; poetry by Yevtushenko, Voznesensky, Zabolotsky, Okudzhava, and Vinokurov. I could keep going with this list with no trouble at all, because the great Italian publishers (Einaudi, Feltrinelli, and Editori Ruiniti) follow our journals very closely and whenever they see anything that interests them, they bring it out literally two or three months later. If only our publishers were as efficient!

And now the movies. We buy many foreign movies. We have seen first-rate pictures by Rosselini, De Sica, Di Santis, Visconti, Fellini, Truffaut, Otan-Lara, Bardem, Karel Zeman, Kavalerovic. But along with these we have had a parade of other things marching across our screen, things that have nothing to do with art: *The Count of Monte Cristo,* two parts of it no less; *Oklahoma!,* and other serenades. We spent money on them that we could have used to buy *Citizen Kane,* which Americans consider the pinnacle of their film art, or *Hiroshima, Mon Amour* by Alain Resnais, or *The Bridge Over the River Kwai* or *Ashes and Diamonds* by Andrzej Wajda, all the films which have be-

48

come milestones in the art of the film around the world.

By the way, speaking of those milestones and of that very Antonioni who was the cause of my red face, what do we know of the heated controversy that is raging now among progressive directors and critics all over the world? What do we know of the debate over two basic directions that the current film is taking, the debate between the Antonioni school, as it has come to be called, and Jean Rouch's school of "Cinema-truth"? Until a little while ago I, for one, knew nothing about it. And it is very interesting.

Right now the Western film is going through a crisis. Little by little, the great Hollywood with its Westerns and horror films is losing its position. Movie attendance has declined rapidly, not without the help of television, of course. In England, in 1961 alone, three hundred movie houses were closed down. In France, in comparison with 1957, the total number of movie-goers declined by 80 million people. Why is this happening? I won't go into great detail, into this very complicated process. I will only quote a little from "The Manifesto of the Young American Film," an appeal to everyone by young American directors, Rogosin, Robert Frank, Bert Stern, the Sandros Brothers and others.

"We want no more glossy finish on our movies," they say. "We would rather have living films, even if they have to be cruel. We want no more films the color of pink rose water. Give us films the color of blood."

Films the color of blood. That is putting it sharply: the choice doesn't have to be between rose water and blood. But the meaning is clear. They are tired of lies and falsehoods. Something new is necessary now, something fresh, contemporary. And so the search for something new is traced out in two directions now. In one, there is Antonioni (and

49

Alain Resnais with his *Hiroshima, Mon Amour* and *Last Year at Marienbad*) and in the other, Jean Rouch and his *The Chronicle of a Summer*.

The Chronicle of a Summer (Rouch was assisted by the sociologist Edgar Morin) is a walk along the streets of Paris with a camera and a microphone. The authors of the film go up to several people—workers, employees, students—and they ask them all a single question: "Are you happy?" They make no attempt to hide the camera or the micro phone: "Just say whatever you want. Don't be bashful. Be yourselves." And the people start talking. The authors gather them all together in the streets, in their homes, in the café. They start arguing different questions: their job, the Algerian War, the Congo. At the end of the picture (it lasts the normal hour and a half), all the people are assembled in a movie studio to see the film, and we see how each one of them reacts to it.

The authors of the film are trying to show absolute truth. They don't hide anything. They don't peep furtively at anything. And they don't set anything up beforehand. They just take people by surprise and, by talking with about a dozen of them, they show us that not one of them is particularly happy. Everyone is worried, everyone is bored with his work, no one gets any satisfaction from it, everyone is concerned most of all with his own problems. Even the rich are bored: the authors meet them at the fashionable resort San Tropez. But at a resort, of course, boredom itself is the fashion.

The film has been the cause of many arguments. Some people have praised it. Others, on the contrary, have said that absolute truth isn't anything you can catch by the tail that way. They say that uninvented characters of the film cannot remain completely natural in front of camera lens simply by virtue of their human characteristics. They are acting, too. Some of them try to seem better, cleverer people than they really are. Others, on the other hand, seem to be advertising their own sincerity. But one way or another, the course that Jean Rouch is taking is an interesting one, even if it is not completely new (remember our own Dziga Vertov * in the twenties). Rouch is engaged in a serious search. He is not alone in this search: in America the directors Shirley Clark (she even brings the camera on the screen in *The Connection*) and Lionel Rogosin are looking in the same direction.

I have seen two of Rogosin's films, *On the Bowery* and *Come Back, Africa*. Together they have brought the director world renown. The first (filmed in 1956) is the story of thirty-year-old American worker, unemployed and fallen to the Bowery, a most awful place in the heart of New York City, where the castaways of life, the alcoholics and the chronically unemployed, wallow in drink. There are no actors in it. Just drunks scattered on the sidewalks; bars, flophouses, prostitutes, brawls, and scuffles: it's all true, all reality, nothing made up. There are only two people in the film who actually play parts (they aren't professional actors but regular inhabitants of the Bowery). These are a young unemployed worker and an old man who is his friend and drinking-mate. The story is very simple: the old man steals a suitcase from his "friend," sells it, and gives part of the money to the very same young worker to get him out of New York. The effect of this film is remarkable. As a document of indictment it has tremendous force.

Come Back, Africa was filmed three years later in the Union of South Africa. Rogosin managed to get there, after

* Soviet director, author of a documentary series called "Cinema-Truth" which ran during the 1920's. (*Translator's note*)

considerable trouble, by pretending that he wanted to film a musical comedy. The comedy didn't turn out to be very gay. It is the sad story of a Negro named Zachariah who comes to make his living in Johannesburg, the great center of the diamond trade. The film is a little long, and there is more craft in it than in the first film. But still there are no actors, and the force of its indictment is just as powerful as *On the Bowery.*

Jean Rouch, Shirley Clark, Rogosin, they are all part of one movement, one direction in the search for truth, using the methods of the documentary film combined with the principles of artistic cinematography. In my opinion, it is a direction which is very interesting and useful.

The other direction is a little more complex. Both Antonioni and Alain Resnais are following it, even if the two of them are hardly cut from the same cloth, and each one has his own brilliantly expressive personality. This is the cinema of something called "anti-drama." This is also a search for truth, but everything you see on the screen is coming to you not from reality, not from the real world, but through the imagination of either the author or the actors. For example, Antonioni believes that reality is so indefinable and elusive that it can be perceived only by intuition. He made that statement in an article I read in *L'Humanité* which dealt with *Eclipse,* the film that won him a special prize at the Cannes Film Festival of 1962. But after I had seen the film, I must say, I couldn't see what he meant. The film is absolutely realistic, and I would even say, truthful in its hopelessness. As no other film I have seen, it reveals the ulcer that is eating away at contemporary civilization in the West, the complete disconnection, alienation, noncommunication (there is such a word in the West now), the inability of people to find a rapport with one another. The acting and the direction are excellent (Alain Delon is in the major role; he was Rocco in *Rocco and His Brothers*). The author's idea is completely clear. But this whole story of the unrealized love of a young stockbroker and a young girl who has once turned down a wealthy lover —this whole story leaves me absolutely cold. It is a matter of complete indifference to me how the story ends. He is a good-looking young man, and she is a good-looking girl, and their kisses are all very suggestive, but I'm not interested. They get together, they drift apart, . . . What do I care? I was much more interested in looking up and down the streets of Rome to recognize a familiar place. In short, I didn't like the picture, even though its social implications are resounding.

Quite the opposite with *Accattone*, Pasolini's film, which I saw twice and liked even better the second time.

The word *Accattone* is untranslatable. We tried it as *The Beggar* or *The Vagabond.** Actually, he is a beggar who wants to get rich, one who uses his comrades in misery for his own advantage. And that's what the film is about, this *accattone,* this Roman *souteneur.* The film itself is very long, very talky, and this is where we Russians have the most trouble with it. The characters speak in a barbaric Roman dialect which is impossible to translate into Russian. I won't tell the story in detail, even though on the surface it's really a very simple one: the *accattone* tries many ways to get himself on his feet; he tries to find a job; but finally he dies. It was filmed very simply. There are no film studios, no sets: it's all taken in the street, in a courtyard, in a bar, apparently, a real bar. There is no artificial lighting, and there are no montages. (By the way, the montage craze is

* The film was produced in England under the original title *Accattone.* (*Translator's note*)

already an anachronism in the West.) But most important, there are no actors. The characters are all cast in their own roles. And what roles they are! Beggars, pimps, prostitutes. Only the *accattone* doesn't play himself: in real life he is Franco Citti, house painter. Finally, as I said before, Pasolini himself is not a professional: this is his first picture.

How do you feel after seeing this picture? You feel as though you had just spent the last two hours with these people. This feeling of actual presence, of your actual presence in the scene, is amazing. There is a lot of neorealism in this, but there is something new in it, too: in the long scenes, in the unmoving camera, in the fact that there are no montages. But it's not a question of methods. You get all the way into the picture. You forget that there is a screen in front of you. That's very important to me when I see a picture; I believe the director and I believe the actors, and therefore I believe what they show me.

Then why can't you call *Accattone* a neorealistic film? In neorealism, too, you get all the way into the picture. There, too, you believe in the director and the actors. And anyway, why do people say now that neorealism has done away with itself?

I don't think it's a question of doing away with itself. It's only that neorealism is such a national phenomenon, so purely Italian (its international influence has been enormous, but in its pure form it has never been reproduced in any other country) that for various reasons its style has undergone a transformation; it has addressed itself to something different now, something narrower.

Neorealism was born right after the war, in a devastated, half-naked, beggarly Italy. It is to this Italy that those films were dedicated; to its people, to the ordinary Romans, the Milanese, the Neapolitans, the workers, peasants, office em-

54

ployees; to the hardship of their everyday life and the nobility of their character; to their ability to help each other in their hour of need. This was the Italy of those films, the films we came to love so much. Now Italy is not that way any more. She has grown strong economically. (Why she has is another question.) And many things about her already show the mark of external prosperity. Maybe it's just because of this (in their art Italians fear any kind of prosperity like the plague) that the attention of the artist has turned to the declassed people, the people who haven't found their place in life—*Nights of Cabiria, Accattone, Rocco and His Brothers*—or on the other hand, to the decayed, hysterically glutted world of *La Dolce Vita*. Possibly, this shift in attention has been a reasonable one, but as the scope of the artist's attention seemed to be getting wider, it was only getting more narrow. On the surface, it is still the same in its authenticity, its truthfulness, its accuracy, but in substance, it is something different, something more private.

And so neorealism has done away with itself. That's what they think in the West anyway. Something new has come to take its place. There are even new terms now, neotraditionalism (Pasolini), neoexperimentalism (Antonioni). But I haven't been able to figure them out yet. I can only say that *Accattone* is an intelligent, serious film, a tragic one (now it's my turn, Pasolini), and a very gifted one. There is a lot of mud in it, both literally and figuratively, but the film itself is pure. A man stumbles, falls, picks himself up, looks for his way out through work, through love, doesn't find it, and dies fleeing from the police. As the *accattone* dies on a dusty bridge, he says, "Now, at last, I'm at peace. . . ." It is a painful film, hopeless, frightening at times, but how much truth there is in it!

The same day I saw *Accattone* (the second time in Moscow) I saw another film, *The Violent Life (La Vie Violente)*, based on a novel by Pasolini but not directed by him. The same Franco Citti and some other actors from *Accattone* act in it and the acting is excellent, but on the whole the film leaves you dissatisfied. Comparing these two films convinced me that when a film is based on a novel, it may have only limited results, but when the screen-writer and director are the same person, the results can be brilliant. After *Accattone* I was finally convinced by *Guard of Lenin* by Marlen Khutsiyev, but more of that later.

A few words on Pasolini's career in films. At the Venice Film Festival of 1962 he showed his second film, *Mama Roma* with Anna Magnani in the leading role. People who saw it say it's an excellent film, a very powerful film. But it didn't receive a prize. (After *Accattone* had made the rounds of every screen in Europe, it finally received a prize at Karlsbad.) There are certain circles in Italy—the church, the police, the upper bourgeoisie—who are out to cause Pasolini every hardship. They don't like him. He takes pictures of the wrong things. They start court actions against him, and they impede his work in any way they can. It reached the point where work on *Mama Roma* almost came to a standstill after the film was already half done. Franco Citti was originally in the leading role. It seems that Citti was drunk one night and got into an argument with the police, which ended in a short scuffle and a year in prison for Franco Citti. If he hadn't been one of Pasolini's actors, his sentence wouldn't have lasted more than ten days. Pasolini had to find another actor and reshoot the film from the beginning. And Citti is sitting in jail. I saw a picture of him with his handcuffs on.

Not long before I saw *Accattone,* literally the day before our departure for Italy, I saw a film by our young Soviet director, Andrey Tarkovsky, *My Name Is Ivan.* If I hadn't seen that first, I would have said that *Accattone* is the way to make a film, or rather that's the way I would make it if I were a director. But after *My Name Is Ivan* I can't say that any more. The strange thing (I've written about this before) is that Tarkovsky's film is composed in a key that is not dear to me by any means. In fact, in many respects it offends me both as a spectator and as someone who has had something to do with making films myself. If in *Accattone* I did not notice the screen at all, here I am always aware of it. There is a lot of craft in *My Name Is Ivan,* a lot of creation, a lot of camera and director's tricks. There is a lot of refined foreshortening, beautiful lighting, sudden transitions and appearances, a lot of especially ambitious designs. The film is not made simply. There is both present and past in it, flash backs and dreams (in *Accattone,* too, by the way) and whole portions of a reality that has not taken place (what might have happened if things had not turned out the way they did). In other words, if I wanted to be hard on this picture, I could say, "God knows what they stuffed into it." And in my opinion, the film has other shortcomings. Every man who has fought in a war is oversensitive about anything that has to do with war. And this film is about war. And, unfortunately, it is not entirely accurate.

But despite all this, in my opinion, this picture by Tarkovsky and his cameraman Yusov, is not only a good picture but a significant one. It is a great, joyous achievement, on the part of the director, the cameraman, and the actors. What is so significant about it and why do I talk about it so

enthusiastically, even though its method is closer to Dovzhenko * than to my beloved neorealism? Because basically
the film has enunciated a truth of human relationships.
And that is very important. This truth is given to us by an
intelligent, talented artist. He is an artist who avoids simplicity, an artist who is always telling us, "Look how I put
this together!" But he is an artist who believes in the people he shows us. And for that reason I believe in them, too.
But I don't believe in the characters in *Poems of the Sea*
or *Stories of the Fiery Years,*** even though they may have
been done by people who are undoubtedly intelligent and
talented.

At the time, I was attacked by no less than a dozen critics
for raising a hand against Dovzhenko in my article "Glorious Words and Simple Words," for canceling out his legacy,
as they said. They said that I am attracted generally to the
mediocre, and if I should ever become a minister of culture—God forbid, as one critic put it—all our film art
would be transformed into something deathly boring and
pedestrian. Fortunately, both for the ministry and for me,
I never became a minister, but in the years that have passed
since I published that article, I have been ultimately convinced that the "glorious words," all the pseudo-pathetic
exaltation, the symbolic meanings, the implausible situa-
tions, the rhetoric, and the wordiness, in short, every attempt to substitute invention for life, all that doesn't reach
the heart of the audience. But on the other hand, the form
of a given picture can even be a negative (for example, in
My Name Is Ivan, or *Last Year at Marienbad*), if only it

---

* A. P. Dovzhenko, Ukrainian director, whose best-known films were
produced in the 1920's and 1930's. (*Translator's note*)
** Films by Dovzhenko. (*Translator's note*)

promotes the thought, and if only the thought is a true one. Tarkovsky's *My Name Is Ivan* convinced me of this.

And now to conclude this discussion of "glorious words" and "simple words," let me quote the following passage from Tolstoy, from "The Raid":

> *The Frenchman at Waterloo who declared, "The guard may perish, but it will never surrender," and other heroes who uttered memorable phrases, mainly Frenchmen, may all have been brave men and they may indeed have uttered memorable phrases. But between the courage of these people and the courage of the captain, there is a difference. Even if my hero had felt a glorious word stirring in his heart, I am sure he would never have uttered it. For one thing, he would have been afraid that by a glorious word he would mar a glorious deed. And secondly, when a man feels the power within himself to perform a glorious deed, no word is necessary. This, I think, is the great, unique feature of Russian courage.*

Why do I talk about the film so much? Not only because I am devoted to it and have even done a little work with it. But because it is really the most massive, the most international, the most accessible form of art, a kind of esperanto, as Pasolini called it. By the way, that congress we went to was devoted especially to the most massive forms of influences on people, the movies and television. But I didn't make a speech at the congress, and now I'm trying to make up for it.

In the little auditorium of the Italy-USSR Society in Rome, I held a showing of a film, *To the Unknown Soldier,* directed by R. Nakhmanovich and produced by the Ukrainian Kinochronic Studies. It is made up of old documentary shorts of the Patriotic War combined with scenes taken now in our own time. It is devoted to the people who fought at the front, to those who worked in the underground, and those who wasted away in Nazi concentration camps, to those who were victorious, and to those—in the words of one of the final scenes—"who gave up their lives so that ours could continue." The film is a documentary from beginning to end, and there is nothing invented in it.

And so, sitting in the auditorium, I watched nervously to see how the Italian audience would react to it. And getting this film across was not easy: I had to translate it on the spot from Ukrainian into Russian so that the interpreter in turn could get it from Russian into Italian. But it got across. By the end of it, I saw that many were in tears.

People cry during sentimental melodramas, I know, but at a documentary they cry a different kind of tears. When you see Kiev in flames through the camera of a German airman; when you see the Kreshchatik * itself exploding into the air; when you see the line of prisoners behind bars in the Stutgof, and these same prisoners (or others just like them) writing their protest on the day that Hoppe, the head of a concentration camp, was freed from prison; when you hear the voice of Viktor Bazhanov grown to be a man now (the last time we saw him he was a ten-year-old boy running around at the front, taking cartridges to his old comrade, Chernobay), when you hear him now, a teacher of physical culture, appealing to all of us to help him find that old friend of his, that Chernobay; when you hear all this, and see it, and remember the past, it is hard to keep calm. It's hard even for me and I wrote the scenario.

* The main boulevard in Kiev. (*Translator's note*)

A documentary film can have enormous power. Remember the Thorndikes' *Operation Teutonic Sword* or *Vacation in Zilte* or *Let Us Not Forget*. What powerful accusations they contain! And Irving Leyser's *Mein Kampf* and *Judgement at Nuremberg* which, by the way, we haven't seen, and still don't understand why not! It is time to tell the story of the Great Patriotic War in the language of a documentary film. It should be a great, serious, truthful document, a chronicle of all our victories and defeats, at home and at the front, the dark days of the occupation, the partisan war, Auschwitz and Baby Yar,* Munich, Nuremberg. . . .

There is a word, *cine-journalism*. Right now it is only a word. It would be good to translate it into action. Volunteers will be found, people to help in this difficult new endeavor, even the Thorndikes ** themselves. I think Jean Rouch's experiment is also interesting. Why don't we try something like that? Something unusual. How much easier it is to shoot those well-rehearsed scenes of production leaders and newly decorated prize winners, with their hair carefully combed and neckties carefully tied, standing by their machines or sitting at enormous desks, preferably against a bookcase for a backdrop, mouthing the words which they learned by heart ahead of time. Why don't we take a camera and a tape recorder and go out into the street, just as Jean Rouch did in Paris? Why don't we go out into Moscow, Kiev, Bratsk, any Soviet city? Why don't we try it?

* A ravine near Kiev where thousands of Jews were slaughtered by the Nazis. It was recently the subject of a controversial poem by Yevgeny Yevtushenko. (*Translator's note*)
** East Germans Andrea and Annelie Thorndike, whose latest documentary, *The Russian Miracle,* has been shown all over the Soviet Union. (*Translator's note*)

How far I've come from where I began. It all began with what I said about arguments. This is how they used to come up. We would start by comparing prices in the Soviet Union and in Italy, and we would end up with the Stanislavsky Method . . . is it living or dead? We would begin in the street and finish in some small *trattoria* in the Trastevere district.

The *trattorias* . . . At the risk of bringing thunder and lightning down upon me, I must sing your praises, sweet Italian *trattoria!* Without you, Italy would be as unthinkable as it would be without oranges, without statues of Garibaldi, and without the white triangular ash trays on your tables that say "Cinzano" or "Martini." If all the *trattorias, osterias,* and bars in Italy were closed for some reason, the Italian would rise in revolt. If such a terrible thing were to happen, where would a poor fellow go to find out the latest news; to have a glass of wine; to play dominoes; to meet pretty Lucia; or Carlo and Alberto, whom he has absolutely got to see for some reason; or just to sit in the corner and think about something that he can't think about at home?

The *trattoria* is not a restaurant. It's more like a club, a meeting place, a place where they are always glad to see you, where they serve you quickly. No, I shouldn't say *serve* you. When you go to the *trattoria,* you feel as though you have just gone over to see your best friend and it's the greatest pleasure for him to take care of you. Oh, if it were only like that in the Abkhazia in Kiev! You go in and you don't smell the rank, meaty odors of the kitchen, and the waitress doesn't snap at you like a she-wolf and tell you, "Wait a minute, it won't kill you. There are many of you and only one of me!" The tablecloths are all clean, and the waitresses don't squabble over forks and knives, and there are no plush curtains with tassels, and no angry, haughty doorman. . . . Oh, how good it would be! Suppose we suggested, as a sort of cultural exchange program for better relations, that our Abkhazia in Kiev should enter into correspondence and a friendly competition with, say, the Buca-Lapi in Florence? They are both fairly small, and they are both in basements. The Buca-Lapi is just a little older; it will be eighty years old this year.

Once a whole group of us went into the Buca-Lapi. You go in through the kitchen, where everything is always sizzling and crackling, but there are no fumes, and no smoke. And then you go into a room with a vaulted ceiling and walls covered from top to bottom with travel and shipping posters. Nothing else, just posters. Italian, French, German, Spanish, American, Argentinian, Mexican. . . . No Russian posters, though.

"Maybe you could send some when you get home," they said. "Then we could hang them right over your table, right where you're sitting now."

Instead, our poets wrote off some humorous verses on post cards, and the proprietor put them right up on the wall.

"Now we have something to remember from the Russians, too," he said.

In return, each one of us received an ash tray as a souvenir of the pleasant time we spent in this nice, friendly little basement. . . .

But, oh, I'm afraid nothing will ever come of my little exchange program, and when the director of the Abkhazia sees what I have written here, I will never be allowed in there again.

Once I said jokingly to Sergio, "Tell me, when communism has triumphed over the whole world, what will you do with the *trattorias?* Will you nationalize them or collectivize them?"

"Well, no," he said. "We won't be in a hurry to do that."

I have a feeling that my little "ode to the *trattoria*" may have made some people feel just the opposite about it.

"Well, so we don't have enough *trattorias* for him," they will say. "Big deal. Italy is not only famous for *trattorias,* and not only for museums. It is a country with a struggling working class, a country of widespread strikes, of unrelieved unemployment, of hardship for the peasants. Why hasn't he said a word about that?"

These future criticisms remind me of something once told me by one of our journalists, not a very intelligent one, who was touring America with me. On the third or fourth day he began to complain.

"When are they going to show us the slums?" he said. "There's nothing to write about—everything is so slick, clean and comfortable."

Somehow I don't want to be like him. We did see slums, and we saw horrible sunless streets in Chicago with the trains roaring by overhead, and in New York we saw the

Bowery with its classic unemployed. And we saw something even worse. We didn't go to the South, but we saw it on television. We saw the Negro children going to school with police escorts to keep them from being torn to pieces by an animal crowd. We saw all that, and it all exists. But if that's all you want to see when you go to a foreign country, why go at all? I am always ashamed when I see people take pleasure in the misfortunes of others. When I see slums, I feel sorry for the people who live in them, and it doesn't give me the slightest pleasure that there still are such terrible houses and barracks in the world, even in the capitalist world which is alien to me.

"I'll be damned," that same journalist told me once. "Did you see that there are two Negroes staying in our hotel? There were even a couple of them in the restaurant today!"

I guess he was offended that these Negroes weren't thrown bodily out of the restaurant. That would have made fine material for an article. In the South the Negroes are thrown out, but that gives me no pleasure whatsoever.

Well, America will be along later. Let's go back to Italy now, to Italian life, and to a subject they talk about in the *trattoria* just as often as they talk about soccer games, or the latest trial of Sicilian monks.

The struggle of the working class, the strikes. . . . I never saw people actually go out into the streets. (I only saw scanty groups of Fascist demonstrators, about thirty young people in cars and motorcycles flapping banners and posters like "Fanfani + Nenni = Togliatti.") But about a year and a half ago, one of the leaders of the Italian Communist party, Alicata, told me something that happened in Genoa in 1960. The Fascist elements tried to organize something like a congress of their own in this large seaport. But the people wouldn't tolerate it. They came pouring out into the streets, most of them young people. Fights broke out, and some shooting, and then the police intervened. There wasn't much about it in our newspapers, but all Italy talked of nothing else. And the interesting part is that the beatniks or *stilyagi*,* youngsters very much like Pasolini's heroes, had a very active hand in the fight against the Fascists.

"These youngsters fought magnificently," Alicata said. "But at present they will only support us when the class struggle is at its sharpest. This is a difficult question, very difficult. It is not a simple matter at all to win them over to our side. They keep to themselves. They don't like to have to follow any leaders. But they hate fascism and they are prepared to fight it to the death. We Communists must consider seriously how we can make use of this seething energy and guide it into the proper channel."

Unfortunately, we were able to visit only one factory during our stay in Italy, a textile plant in Prato, near Florence. As far as its technical process is concerned, compared to the Olivetti enterprises which I had seen on my previous trip to Italy, this factory was not very interesting. We listened to a not-very-demanding explanation by one of the directors, and we asked the appropriate number of questions. Then we drank a glass of vermouth, had a tour of one of the departments, and exchanged a few words with some workers, even had our pictures taken with them. Finally, as always, we went to the mayor's house to have another drink and see beautiful paintings by Filippino Lippi, bas-reliefs by Donatello and majolicas by Andrea della Robbia.

But everything isn't as quiet as that in every factory. The very day we were visiting the textile mill at Prato,

---

* Soviet teenagers most easily recognized by a leather jacket, tight pants, and a rebellious nature. (*Translator's note*)

there were talks being held in Rome between the new government and representatives of the General Confederation of Italian Labor in an attempt to halt the walkout at the Michelin Plant in Turin, one of Italy's largest producers of automobile tires. The strike had lasted since January. The management had tried to establish a lockout, but nothing did any good, not even strikebreakers. By the end of the second month, management was forced to give in. The workers, who hadn't received a lira during those two months, were victorious at last. And it's no exaggeration to say that the whole city had come to their help. A solidarity committee was organized. They collected money in the stadiums and the markets, even in the streets. One of the largest theaters in town donated the proceeds of several performances to help the workers' cause.

All this tells us a great deal. And it's not an isolated instance. Strikes are widespread phenomena, in the factories, among office workers, railroad and postal employees, the agricultural workers of the South. And as a rule management doesn't come off the winner. Italy is a country with an active political struggle, a country where the working class and the Communist party (of almost two million members) must be taken into account.

Italy is going through an economic upsurge. And that's true not only of Italy, but the German Federal Republic and Japan, all the defeated countries of the last war. The standard of living in Italy has noticeably risen: in the last five years wages have increased significantly, unemployment has fallen, housing construction has expanded on a mass scale, and more and more Italian products are being sold on the world market. What is responsible for it?

There are many causes. Here are the main ones: In the first place, Italy's industrial equipment was almost entirely replaced after the war. Replacing old machinery is never a very easy matter in peacetime, but in Italy it didn't come about simply as a luxury: most of Italy's factories had been completely destroyed. As a result, industrial technology in Italy has now reached a very high level. In the second place, like the other defeated nations, Italy was deprived of her colonies and therefore relieved of the burden of colonial wars. And finally, Italy's military budget is relatively low: she doesn't need to spend money on rockets because America generously provides them for her under the auspices of NATO.

All this has led to a state of the economy which people in the West call "the economic miracle." One should add also that in this given stage capitalism is forced to develop new forms in the relationship of management and labor ("Neo-capitalism," "People's capitalism," "Social partnership," "Olivetti paternalism"), but that would require a special treatment that has no place in sketches that make no claim to a scientific approach.

Where will things go from here? I won't try to answer that question either. As far as Italy is concerned, I think it depends not on what happens in the country itself but rather on what happens beyond her borders. We live in a world in turmoil. And what happens on the streets of Algiers, at the Brandenburg Gate, at Cape Canaveral, and in the corridors of the New York Stock Exchange, will play a part in the future of every Turin factory worker, every Roman schoolboy, and every farm hand in Lucania.

Now I want to tell the story of a young Italian from the town of Carpi, near Modena, whom I met in Moscow in the fall of 1961. This is how it happened.

There is a factory in Carpi that makes woolen shirts famous all over Italy. And the director of this factory is a man named Benito Gualdi, a generous, capricious man. By nature, I would even say, a democratic man. In this town of Carpi, as in all Italian towns, there are gas stations as well as factories. And in one of these gas stations, there is a young and very lively young fellow working as an attendant, Danilo Cremasci.

Italians are a sociable people and, as I said before, they love to go to the *trattoria* and argue about all kinds of things. And so at one of these *trattorias,* an argument took place between Benito and Danilo.

It started over the fact that Gualdi had recently been to the Soviet Union. He had come as a tourist. But he didn't like our country. And instead of the two weeks he had planned to spend with us, he stayed just four days and made off for Spain or Portugal. Why didn't he like our country? For many reasons, many important reasons. In the first place, in the Ostankino Hotel, where he was staying, none of the clocks were working. Secondly, there were very few taxis in Moscow and no other cars. Thirdly, the cashiers in stores used abacuses instead of cash registers. Fourthly, housewives in Moscow have to keep their pots and pans locked up in communal kitchens. And so on, things like that. . . .

Benito was telling all about it in the *trattoria* with great gusto, and people were listening to him with open mouths. But Danilo was outraged.

"That's a lie," he said.

"It's not a lie."

"I say it's a lie."

"And I say it isn't."

"All right, then, prove it."

"What do you mean prove it? I saw it myself."

"But *I* didn't. How do *I* know?"

"What you mean, how do *you* know?"

"Maybe you're making it up."

"Making it up? All right then, go see it for yourself."

"How am I going to do that?"

"I'll tell you. You go to the Soviet Union, and I'll pay your expenses."

"You'll pay my expenses?"

"That's right."

"You'll pay for the whole trip?"

"The whole trip, hotels, everything!"

"Well what the hell then, I'll go!"

And so he went.

It sounds made up, doesn't it? But Danilo did go to the Soviet Union. I saw him here myself. I don't remember what they had at stake, but Danilo was to confirm or refute everything Gualdi had seen, and when he came back he was to give an honest account of everything. And so, surrounded by friends and reporters, Danilo Cremasci, gas-station attendant from the town of Carpi, got on the train for Moscow and set out for parts unknown.

He spent ten days in Moscow, ten days full of all kinds of "programs." Theaters, museums, clubs, meetings, and more reporters on top of it all. He was a young fellow, full of energy, on his first trip to Moscow, and he ran around from morning to night like a squirrel on a treadmill. Writing! Writing! Writing! He filled up a whole stack of notebooks. He went to the Ostankino, to have a look at the clocks (they were all stopped); he counted the number of taxis in the streets, looked over the Moscow cashier girls. . . . In short, he was up to his neck in work. And he liked it.

"When I get home," he chuckled, "I'll have a few things to tell them."

On his last day in Moscow, some friends of mine and I had a drink with him and a friend of his, Corrado Sacci, an Italian student at Moscow University. We had a farewell drink in his room at the Hotel Berlin, we put them in a taxi and then, waving back at us, they were off for the station.

How the story ended, I don't know. The silence of the bourgeois newspapers bespeaks a victory for Danilo. I didn't see Danilo when I was in Italy. I didn't go to Carpi or Modena, and probably Danilo didn't even know of our arrival. But a little while ago, I received a post card with two lines on it, best regards, and two signatures: Danilo Cremasci and Corrado Sacci. Sacci comes from the same town, and probably he was home on vacation.

An amusing story, isn't it? And so thoroughly Italian.

Incidentally—and this is just in passing—on one of those autumn days I took Danilo and Corrado with another friend of mine to Zagorsk,* to the Trinity-Sergian Lavra.** We thought they would find it interesting to see what the religious situation is here, especially since they come from a country where the church is so strong. And, of course, the architecture at Zagorsk is really remarkable.

And so we all went out there together. But my friend and I turned out to be much more amazed by what we saw than our Italian friends. Plainly, they were used to fanaticism and religious zeal in their own country, and nothing like that could surprise them. But my friend and I couldn't believe our eyes.

And who would have thought it? A hundred kilometers or so from the center of Moscow, there still exists an authentic chapter out of deaf, hoary, dreadful pre-Petrine Rus. . . . There are countless old women, all in black, fleshless, nasty, and malevolent. They roam around the courtyard. They loiter in the churches, muttering under their breath. And they stand in line for hours to kiss the remains of St. Sergius of Radonezh.

We have a hard time getting into the church, attacked from all directions by scorching hostility. Inside it is crowded and gloomy; an arched ceiling hanging low, the hissing of candles. From the walls the stern faces of saints gaze down at us. At the shrine, holding the relics, the sleek, good-looking figure of a priest. The line of people winds on silently, men among them, even young people. Every-

* A town near Moscow which dates from the fourteenth century. Russian believers travel great distances to worship there. (*Translator's note*)
** One of the four ancient monasteries in Russian Orthodoxy, which by virtue of size and importance were given the name of *lavra*. (*Translator's note*)

one makes the sign of the cross, and bends low over the relics. And they all hate us. They despise us.

"Unbelievers! Heathens!"

Out in the yard again, there are crows circling in the limpid autumn sky above the breath-taking cupolas. And below, near the white walls of the cathedral, hysterical hags are swarming around the bloodless, emaciated body of a *yuridivo* * with huge rolling eyes. They keep pouring water over his head, and he, wet and miserable, caresses the hair of a young woman who clings to him, gazing at her with enraptured eyes, mumbling his prophecies.

"There will be no war. No war. Live in peace, love each other. That's the most important thing—love. Look to me no longer, I won't answer you. I won't answer you even if you ask. You have an evil eye. Get away from me, away, away.

"Yes, the end of the church is near. The church is living its final hours. Pray. Pray to God. Evil days are upon us. War is drawing near, there will be slaughter, and life on earth will come to an end, and only flowers will live on, and leaves, and grass, and the sky and the sea, and ask me no more. I can say no more. Beginning today, from this Sunday forward, I will say nothing. I will be silent for a whole year, for two years, three years. . . ."

But the women flocking around him cried:

"No, no. Tell me. My dear one, my own, speak to me. To me."

But their dear one, their own one, only holds tighter to the girl clinging to him, and then suddenly they begin to rub noses, hurriedly, ecstatically. . . . It is frightening.

* A person thought to be beloved of God and to possess visionary powers, often suffering from a mental or nervous disorder. (*Translator's note*)

A young woman wanders about the courtyard, skinny and black like the others. She wrings her hands and mumbles. Mumbles about the end of the church, mumbles about deception, about lack of faith. . . .

We were in the center of orthodoxy, and we didn't find it merciful, loving, and God-fearing, but something evil and hateful. There was a dark dangerous power in it, a power which still exists right in the midst of us.

Long will I remember that autumn day: those black old women with their bundles; the shivering fool of God; the sleek, healthy, handsome movements of the priests; the velvet tones of the deacon. And the crows, swarms of crows in a clear sky. And the hatred.

I remembered it a half a year later, in Italy, as I stood on the square in front of St. Peter's Cathedral, waiting for the Pope to appear. Every Sunday exactly at twelve o'clock he comes to his window and gives his blessing to the faithful. And the enormous, colonnaded square is full of people.

When it was twelve o'clock and the tiny figure of Pope John XXIII made an appearance, white against the long red cloth that was draped from his window, many people fell to their knees. He gave a short sermon which carried over the square by dozens of loud-speakers, then raised his hands to the sky, and disappeared. Some people in automobiles blew their horns in salute.

And although I saw a lot of kneeling people around me —among them many young monks and nuns in all colors of habit and complexion—all praying to the lord God, still there was something "modern" in all this. As soon as the Pope had disappeared, everyone started talking about his own worldly affairs, including the monks; and nimbly dodging the traffic, the crowd moved gaily and noisily down the broad Via Conciliazione.

The power and influence of the Catholic Church is enormous, I know. And religious fervor in Italy can often take monstrous forms (remember the church scenes in *Nights of Cabiria,* even though they were noticeably cut for our showing). But compared to what I saw at Zagorsk, that Sunday encounter with the Pope seemed just a colorful spectacle, something planned by the Grandi-Viaggi Tourist Company.

By the way, to some extent, this modernity of the contemporary Catholic Church is its new weapon. Its way of influencing the faithful is changing. Even the Pope is not what he used to be. For example, people say (I'm going by the Italian newspapers) that Pope John XXIII at eighty was a very democratic man: he would sit at table with his chauffeur and even take a glass of wine with him. The Pope believed in peaceful coexistence. After the launching of Vostok III, he held a special service at his summer place at Castel Gandolfo, in Nikolayev's honor. Everything is in flux. Everything is changing.

The time has finally come to deal in closer detail with the congress of the European Society of Writers, which was the real reason for our trip.

It was a well-attended and representative congress, and almost all of the newspapers of the world reported it. There were about four hundred writers present from every European country except Albania (which is not a member of the Society) and the German Democratic Republic, which was prevented from sending representatives by the American command in Berlin. In the assembly halls and corridors you could meet Halldor Laxness from tiny far-away Iceland; or Guisseppe Ungaretti, just elected president of the association to succeed Gianbattista Angioletti; the young but already well-known Juan Goytisolo; or cheerful Marie Marejova, still interested in everything in spite of her eighty years; or Marguerite Duras, author of *Hiroshima, Mon Amour;* Nazim Hikmet, representing Turkish literature; Jaroslaw Iwaszkiewicz, André Chamson, Cesare Giavattina, and many, many others. The representatives of Algeria and Cuba were greeted with ovations. Even Fanfani was supposed to be there, but a change in his cabinet prevented him from coming, and Minister Codacci-Pizanelli addressed the congress in his place and made the presentation of a "small gift" from the Italian government, namely the famous Villa Petraia which is now the permanent residence of the Society.

The congress was devoted to the role and meaning of literature in radio, television, and the film. That was its "agenda," so to speak. But actually, the unifying principle of the congress was the anti-fascism it so clearly expressed, its support of the struggle for peace and the development of closer relations between West and East. In our difficult age, the hardest thing of all is to get together and talk, to talk as frankly and openheartedly as possible. And not only from the rostrum . . .

The correspondent of the *Il Matino* was right when he wrote (and many other papers wrote the same thing): "I can't tell you where the real congress took place, whether it was in the Hall of the Five Hundred, in the rooms adjoining it, the corridors of the hotel, or in the streets of Florence when the furious gusts of wind died down. The important thing is that writers of different countries are meeting, talking, and getting to know each other. In a way, the work of the congress is just an excuse for that."

Yes, it really was, just that.

But let us return to our "agenda." There were speeches about literature, television, the film, about what holds them all together. There were many opinions, often diametrically opposed. Marguerite Duras declared that "the film has nothing in common with literature. The conception of time in the novel does not correspond in any way to the conception of time in the film." She said that as far as her own film was concerned, she had never once been present at the shooting of a scene, and she never let the director have anything to say about the scenario. Despite her success with *Hiroshima, Mon Amour*, Marguerite Duras announced that she would never do another film. And the French writer Bernard Pengo said something to the same effect.

But as all the Italian papers agreed, the most interesting speech at the congress was Grigori Chukhrai's. He was a star of the first magnitude, and the crowds of correspondents never gave him a moment's peace.

On the sixteenth of March, *Unita* wrote: "Chukhrai is the outstanding figure at the congress. His speech against exploiting eroticism in films released a veritable storm. The Soviet director has suffered fairly harsh treatment. He had found himself applauded by the conservative and clerical press and censured by liberals as a moralist. Yesterday, he was attacked from the rostrum of the congress by the writer Repaci, and today he was defended by Pasolini."

The fact is that in Italy now the Church and the progressive intelligentsia, including the Communists, are fighting a fierce battle over what is permissible in the film. Chukhrai spoke of the moral purposes of art, and the clerical circles tried to turn his speech to their own advantage. The next day, the newspaper *Paese* carried an interview between Chukhrai and one of their correspondents.

"Listen to me carefully," Chukhrai said. "If you had listened to me carefully in the first place, you would have understood that I am not defending conformists and I am not supporting the morality of hypocrites. I allow the artist's prerogative to deal with any subject he pleases and to depict reality with complete freedom. I was only speaking against the exploitation of the sexual aspect of love."

But the fighting over Chukhrai's speech didn't die down for a long time. For a long time, his picture was always in the papers. And *Ballad of a Soldier,* "fundamentally naïve and sentimental," according to Pasolini, drew capacity audiences just as before and gave the Italian movie-goer a lot to think about.

The congress lasted four days. For four days it was boisterous and noisy in the Hall of the Five Hundred, in the corridors around it, and on the ancient staircases, guarded by soldiers with halberds. If you had been there during those four days, you would have been sure to see a short, lively man about forty years old, darting here and there, talking to people, starting an argument, then darting off again to talk to somebody else. It was La Pira, the Mayor of Florence, one of the most interesting and original figures in Italy today.

La Pira is a convinced Catholic. More than that, he is the ideological leader of the Catholic left wing. He is close to the Pope, and a friend of Fanfani's. He initiated the meeting between the mayors of all European capitals, held in Florence in 1955 for the sole purpose of uniting them in the struggle for peace. He was an active supporter of the Algerian people in their fight for independence. And not only the Algerian people: every people in Africa considers him a friend. He is not a monk, but he lives like one, in a Franciscan monastery. He is honest and unselfish, and very active. If it hadn't been for him, there would have been no congress. As mayor of the city, he spared nothing to get it organized. And, indeed, he was the heart of the congress itself, one of its most active members.

At the final meeting, this is what he said:

"When you return to your countries and they ask you there what news you bring from Florence, tell them, 'Excellent news!' You can give them the hope that there will be no more war. Nuclear disarmament will be accomplished, the prophesy of Isaiah will be fulfilled. They shall beat their cannons into ploughshares, their missiles into spaceships. Peace is close upon us. The first sign of that peace is the cease-fire between the Algerians and the French. . . . The civilization of the future will be a civilization of dialogue.

"Florence has made you all her honorary citizens, and she bids you take brotherly greetings to the capitals of your nations, which concluded a pact of peace and friendship with her on the fourth of October, 1955. I urge you to visit the mayors of your capitals and tell them that Florence has been true to the pact of peace and friendship which they concluded with her seven years ago. Tell them Florence invites them to visit her again and waits to receive them in the name of that treaty of hope."

And if La Pira was the heart of the congress, its soul was Vigorelli, the general secretary of the Society and editor of the magazine *Europa Letteraria*. He was effervescent, everywhere at once. He managed to get four hundred European writers under the arches of the Palazzo Vecchio with only three people to help him, and as we might say, "their life there was brilliantly organized." I remember when Vigorelli came to the Soviet Union a few years ago and stopped for a day at Irpen. People were still talking about the European Society of Writers in abstract discussions over coffee cups on the veranda. Now it has come into being, and as we can see, it has completely justified itself. Its members are more than a thousand writers from many different countries. And for all of this, the great credit goes to one man—a man who is always cheerful and energetic even though he got a little tired by the end of the congress, a man who is editor, critic, public figure, and an interesting and lively conversationalist at the same time—to Gian-Carlo Vigorelli.

At the congress I saw a count I knew, the writer Guido Piovene, with whom I had wandered two years earlier through the snowy alleys of Maleyvka, near Moscow. Then, dressed in his fur coat and cap, he continued his journey to Siberia, which he described in a series of articles. Now, standing at the podium of the congress, he said:

"For the first time, peace seems to us an absolute good, and everything depends on it. As a result, for the first time in history, the love of peace and the preservation of peace have become inseparable from artistic creation."

Unfortunately, Renato Guttuzo was not at the congress. He is one of the greatest painters in Italy, a kind, gracious, and remarkably simple man. Last year when he came to the Ukraine as Bazhan's guest, I had the pleasure of introducing him to some Kiev painters, Zinoviev Tolkachevy, and the two youngsters, Ada Rybachuk and Vladimir Melnichenko, whose works he praised very highly. At that time there was an exhibit of Guttuzo's works in Moscow, but I couldn't get to see it, so now, in Italy, I was looking forward to the pleasure of seeing his paintings in his studio. But I couldn't do that either. While the congress was going on, Guttuzo was in London, attending an exhibit of his works.

But I did have the pleasure of meeting at the congress Juan Goytisolo, who came with the delegation of Spanish and Portuguese writers. Not all these writers can live in their native land (Goytisolo, for example, is obliged to live in Paris). But their voices can still be heard, strong and clear, and no Franco or Salazar can suppress them. I was very sorry that our meeting was confined to sitting at the same table during one of the series of receptions. Of course, I was glad we met at least that once, but I very much wanted to see them again. For people of my generation, who well remember the heroic days of the defense of Madrid, everything about Spain—the University City, Velasquez' house, Manzanares, and Carabanchel, Alto and Bajo—has been near and dear to us since then. That is why I hoped that our meeting could last longer than the warm *brudershaft* which we drank with Juan Goytisolo.

In Florence I saw my old friend Vittorio Strada. We began our acquaintance by correspondence in 1955—he translated my novel *Home Town*—and we became friends when he came to study in Moscow. Now I was happy to embrace him in his native Italy. He is a great specialist on Russian and Soviet literature, one of the greatest in Italy. He works in Turin now, at the Einaudi publishing house; it is thanks to his knowledge and his ability that the Italian reader can know our prose and poetry in good translations. We saw each other quite often while I was in Florence, and how good it was to see Vittorio cheerful and gay, even though at the same time, out of a certain patriotic egotism, I was glad to see that he missed Russia a little. He spent four years here, and although he brought home a Russian wife with him, still I could see he missed a lot of what he left behind.

You can't count all the people I was glad to meet, all the people I walked with along the streets of Rome and Florence. I saw all my friends at the Italy-USSR Society, Lizu Foa and Umberto Cherroni, and Pietro Tsveteremich, sprinkled as always with cigarette ashes. (He was the one who shared with me the task of translating *To the Unknown Soldier* from Ukrainian to Russian to Italian.) And Angello Rippelino, who took us to see the very talented young painter Achille Perilli, whose paintings were set aside in a separate exhibition hall at the last Venetian Biennale. By the way, as I looked at the prospectus of his latest exhibit, I couldn't help thinking of Ada Rybachuk and Vladimir Melnichenko. It's true that they are younger than Perilli (he is thirty-five, and they are both about thirty), but he has already had five individual exhibits and, in addition, his work has been shown as part of twenty-seven group exhibits both in his own country and abroad —in Prague, Paris, Vienna, Monaco, Copenhagen, Stockholm, Oslo, Berlin, Melbourne, twice in New York, Mexico, San Francisco, Düsseldorf, Rome, and Brussels. Our young Kievans—and let me say it again, they are very talented—have never had their own exhibits. This year they were invited to give an individual exhibit in Prague, but the Artists' Union of Kiev imposed its "veto."

"Young people," it said, "it's too early for you. For the time being, you must work."

And for an artist, even a young artist, it is so important to have an exhibit, so necessary.

I went to Carlo Levi's studio and saw the paintings he selected for his exhibit in Moscow. And I saw Irina Coletti (she was a Malysheva, Russian by descent). Last winter, she and I had walked around the Kremlin together, and along the snowy side streets of the Arbat district, and I showed her the old house on the corner of Gagarin and Khrushchev streets (quaint old names, aren't they?) where the masons used to hold their meetings and even Pushkin used to come. And now she was taking me around the streets of Rome and showing me an old Franciscan church with walls and ceilings faced with human bones and skulls. . . .

And we saw Giorgio Pastore, a cheerful, lively person who knows Rome as no one else does. I had seen a lot of him, in Rome, Moscow, and Kiev. He spent many years in the Soviet Union and speaks good Russian, and so we found it easiest and simplest to be with him. He drove us around Rome in his car, and then he took us to dinner at the "Old America" where they roast the entire carcass of a sheep or God knows what on a spit in the middle of the room, and a chef in a white hat puts the garnish on the platters with both hands, and the waiters scurry among the tables with Smith-Wessons slapping against their sides, like real cowboys. And we saw young men dancing the twist for money with middle-aged "ladies" and "signoras." (By the way, when young people dance the twist together, it is a very engaging sight; I might even say a beautiful one.) And then Giorgio took us to the Passagiatta Archeologia—the very place where Cabiria had the fight with her colleague—and right before our eyes, two police cars drove up and the "girls" waiting for their customers by the ancient walls of the Baths of Caracalla scattered in all directions. And on Sunday, Giorgio asked us to go to the mountains with him, to go skiing. What a tempting thought, to go skiing in Italy. But we didn't want to leave Rome, and so we refused.

We had another guide for our stay in Rome, Alberto, a film producer, as he called himself. We enjoyed together the view from the Aventine Hill, of a twilit Rome spreading away at our feet. Then, swinging open the giant gates, we looked into the Lozhi Park of the Knights of Malta. And we strolled along the quiet walks of the English cemetery near the pyramids of Caio Cestio and plucked a flower of remembrance from the graves of Shelley and Keats. . . . And then Alberto showed us ancient and medieval Rome. It was a cold, rainy day, and at the corner of a narrow, winding little street, there was a bonfire kindled, with colorful old women and boys warming themselves

84

next to it. I took a picture of them, and they smiled. And when they found out we were Russians—*Sovieticos*—they wanted to see my camera.

And on the very last day, I roamed around the city with Marcello, the same Marcello I had roamed with when I was last in Italy, the one who used to say, whenever we would drive past any kind of ancient church, "Look, there's a *babushka!*" Unfortunately, I didn't have his address, and he had changed his job in the meantime: now he was working on the editorial board of the newspaper *Paese*. And so I reached his office only the day before we left. He wasn't there, and so I left him a note in the garage: he was to be on duty that night.

The next day, early in the morning, he showed up in his car.

"*Ciao,* Viktor!"

"*Ciao,* Marcello!"

He hadn't changed at all. He was still the same black-eyed, curly-haired Marcello, with the bright white smile, just as gay and friendly. The only difference those five years had made to him were two little boys, each one just as black-eyed and curly-haired as he. He had two little pictures of them framed under the windshield of his car, and under the frame there was an inscription, "Don't speed, Papa!" I pestered him so much that he finally gave me these pictures, and now they face me on my table: two wonderful curly-haired young boys, whom unfortunately I have never seen.

Marcello came with us to find presents and souvenirs for our friends in Kiev and Moscow. And that wasn't hard, really. There is an enormous book market right opposite the Termini Station, with everything from comics to splendidly printed art books. We mainly bought reproductions. There are hundreds of them there, if not thousands. There are big ones on canvas, done by a very ingenious process, and small ones, about the size of a cigarette pack, made out of some kind of break-proof and scratch-proof plastic. There are heaps of them on the counters—Van Goghs, Giottos, Rubens, Botticellis, Hokusais, Cezannes, Klees, Mantegnas, Raphaels, Claude Monets, Matisses. You could stand there all day picking them out. It's both a pleasant and an agonizing job, when you don't have that much money, and you want to buy everything you see. But these little reproductions aren't expensive at all: 500 lire each. That's about as much as a seat at the movies, or a little more than a pack of Chesterfield cigarettes.

(A few words about prices. Everyone, both in Italy and in Russia, is always asking how much everything costs. And it's very hard to answer. For example, an average dinner with wine is 1,000 lire, a good pair of shoes from a "bargain-counter" is 1,500 lire, a bottle of wine 300 lire, an ordinary but decent suit is 15,000 to 20,000 lire, a beautifully printed book with illustrations in color is 10,000 or 15,000 or 20,000 lire. A Bible in any language is 1,700 lire, a used car 200,000 lire, a new Fiat 600,000 to 650,000 lire. Now try to figure it out. . . .)

We got back to the hotel loaded down with reproductions and some ceramic work. (Next to the book mart there is a special store where the amateur collector can spend an entire fortune, but by that time we were already out of money.) Then we went to the embassy, and then to Carlo Levi's studio, and then Marcello left us. We didn't see him that evening because his wife wasn't feeling well, but he came the next day to drive us to Fuimichino Airport.

In one day, our whole group had come to like Marcello. Saying good-by to him was like saying good-by to an old friend. He bid me a Georgian farewell by giving me his little striped cap for a keepsake. (Quite innocently I happened to tell him once: "What a nice cap you have, Marcello!") And then shaking everybody's hand he pronounced in his Russo-Franco-Italian language:

"Until next year. In 1963 I will come to the Soviet Union. It is already decided. *Arrivederci,* Moscow! Until we meet again in Moscow!"

"And in Kiev."

"In Kiev. In Kiev . . ."

The four-engine "Viscount" was already rolling down the runway, but Marcello was still standing there waving. And we were still waving too. In his person, we were bidding good-by to Italy, to all the friends we had there.

Below us the green-blue Tyrrehenian Sea was gently rippling, and then the island of Elba floated by, jagged with coves. And we all thought how great it would be when Marcello came next year in his Alfa-Romeo. Then we would drive around the streets of Kiev instead of Rome, and as we drove past the Cathedral of St. Sophia, I would say, "Look, Marcello, there's a *babushka!*"

There is only one thing that worries me, and that is how Marcello would fare with the Kiev police. Like a true Roman, he has complete contempt for traffic lights, and likes to drive at seventy-five miles an hour. Anyway. I have some past experience in these matters, and I think—even if Marcello is not the son of a president—we will manage to get out of it somehow.

AMERICA

My first experience with America took place forty years ago in my native Kiev, in the bare and difficult year of 1922. I was eleven years old then and I used to run around barefoot (rope-soled shoes and wooden clogs were an unheard of luxury). And I went to the fifth grade of Labor School Number 43.

We used to call it the United States of North America, and I knew it mostly through Mayne-Reed * and Fenimore Cooper, through postage stamps (the pictures of the Presidents were not very interesting) and through the condensed milk which we children were suckled on by Hoover's American Relief Administration. It was a great thrill for us to collect the labels on the cans, with their pictures of Indians and buffaloes. In addition, on my way to school I used to see copies of *Proletarskaya Pravda* pasted along the walls; and I used to stop and try to make out the news (it was printed on blue wrapping paper)

* A British-born contemporary of Cooper, who also wrote about the American wilderness. Though little known in the West, together with Cooper he has been staple reading in Russia before and after the revolution. (*Translator's note*)

about the Greco-Turkish war and the Washington conference. I hadn't been to any American movies yet. That
came the next year, with *The Empress of the World, The
Queen of the Forests,* and *The Goddess of the Jungle.* And
I had never set eyes on a live American. At the ARA, the
milk and the snow-white rolls, soft as cotton, were handed
out by Russians.

And then one fine day in Kiev a guest came to stay with
us, none other than the Director of the New York Public
Library, Mr. Harry Miller Lydenberg. There were no
hotels in town, and at that time, I had an aunt who was
working in the library of the Academy of Sciences, so he
came to stay with us. He was a lean, middle-aged man, and
he carried a portable typewriter strapped across his shoulders. Every day he used to peck out a long letter home on
it, and when he came to the end of each line, a little bell
would ring, so at first I was getting up every minute to see
who was at the door. As soon as he arrived, we prepared a
bath for him. That was not an easy matter because there
was no firewood and sometimes there wasn't even any
water. And so we were very proud of our well-appointed
bath, with our clean towel all set out for him. But in two or
three minutes our guest came out again without touching
either the water or the towel. We were all disappointed.

After dinner he offered to help us with the dishes—he
said he always did that at home—but we wouldn't let him.
After he'd gone, we found a dollar pinned to his pillow,
a dollar or a ten-rouble note, I don't remember which.
We were all a little offended, and at the same time we were
touched. And that's all I remember about Harry Miller
Lydenberg, the director of one of the largest libraries in
the world. The first American I ever met. I liked him.

My second American worked on the construction of the railroad station. I was working there, too, as an apprentice, after I was through with trade school. His name was Borkgravink, but the workers called him *Borschtgrivennik* * because he stood patiently in line with everyone else in the workers' mess, waiting for his plate of borscht. He was tall and thin and taciturn, and he wore thick-soled shoes, which were the objects of general envy. As consultant specialist on concrete, he used to write out a memorandum every day—"A Memo from Mr. Borkgravink"—which was hung in the office of the project director. I didn't like this American very much. I found him rather a bore.

After that I met no more Americans, unless you count General Sherman, a medium tank I had one ride on at the front. A good many years went by, and then in the fall of 1960, or more precisely, on November 2, 1960, at 9:30 P.M. New York time, I first stood on American soil, or rather on American concrete, at Idlewild International Airport.

Whatever you say, I think it's amazing. In one day you can get halfway round the earth. In the morning we were in frosty, snowy Moscow, and twenty hours later we were carrying our coats over our arms, in New York City.

About halfway, we landed in Brussels. Beside our lunch, we took in the ancient halls of the Hotel de Ville and inspected the Atomium, now abandoned. Then in fifteen minutes, we were flying over the English Channel. "Look! Look!" London was somewhere off on our right, they said, but you couldn't see anything. Then Manchester, covered with light as far as you could see. And Ireland, dark as night. Silent Shannon, where we took on the last European

* Literally, Borsht-Penny. (*Translator's note*)

passengers. And then on for seven hours over the ocean. We dozed off in the half-empty "Intercontinental." Then suddenly, we woke up again to a Columbus-like cry:

"Land!"

After Manchester, there was nothing special about the lights of New York: there must have been a light haze over the city.

That night from my window on the twentieth floor of the Governor Clinton Hotel I looked out over Pennsylvania Station below me, at the glittering sign on the editorial office of *The New Yorker*,* and I still didn't believe my eyes. Am I really in New York?

I anticipate a thousand questions. Is it true that the Ku Klux Klan terrorizes everybody? Is it true that in New York a crime is committed every six minutes? Is it true that in the summer the temperature goes up to 100° degrees in the shade? Is it true that one in every four Americans owns a car. Is it true, is it true . . . ? No, I won't answer any questions like these. I will only tell about those things which I saw with my own eyes. And I won't use any statistics either, if I can help it, even though they love statistics so much in America. Or maybe just because they do.

Let me begin with New York. No, I'll begin with our group. We were not a delegation, we were tourists. There were twenty of us: teachers, journalists, engineers, what is called the Soviet intelligentsia. Each one of us had paid out a round sum of money, and in return we were to be taken around the northeastern states by train and bus, to New York, Washington, Chicago, Niagara Falls, Detroit, Dearborn, Buffalo, and back to New York again. The leader of

* What Nekrasov saw was the red neon sign on top of the Hotel New Yorker across Pennsylvania Station from the Governor Clinton Hotel. (*Translator's note*)

our group was a fine person—let us call him Ivan Ivanovich
—but he was very timorous: you would think he had been
frightened of something ever since his childhood. In addition, we had a guide assigned to us by the American Express
Travel Company, a lively, self-assured man in a bow tie,
Tadeusz Osipowicz, an emigré from Poland or the Baltic
area. Let me say right now that he had nothing in common
with Mr. Adams of *Little Golden America.**

Of course, it would be naïve to think you can get an idea
of America in two weeks. What you can do is compare what
you see with what you have read about before. And, of
course, it all depends on how the trip is organized.

Let me say straightaway that the Soviet tourist is not allowed to go everywhere. The South was not included in our
itinerary: New Orleans, Louisiana, Mississippi, the places
where the Negro problem is much more complicated than
it is in the North. In New York, Brooklyn is strictly off
limits. At Niagara Falls any taxi driver will offer to drive
you to the Canadian side for a dollar or so; there is a particularly good view of the falls from there. But Tadeusz
Osipowicz warned us not even to think of it.

America is a special country. A Soviet woman writer who
visited it said what struck her most about America was that
"there was nothing striking about it." Somehow I don't believe that. A great many things struck me, anyway, even
though I was prepared for a lot of what I saw: the skyscrapers, the vast numbers of cars, the lights of Broadway
and the Sunday papers that weigh over two pounds. But it
is these very things—the gigantic buildings, the gigantic
cities, the superhighways cutting across the whole country

* The good-natured guide who accompanied the satirists Ilf and Petrov on
the American tour they described in their travel book *Little Golden America.* (*Translator's note*)

with streams of cars flowing over them, the twenty-story department stores, the endless bacchanalia of advertisements, all the external wealth and abundance that overwhelm you immediately—these are what prevent you from getting to the deeper and more fundamental things.

For to get down to the essentials, to see the country in any depth, you need to do more than tour museums, or go up to the top of the Empire State Building, or take pictures of Niagara Falls. You need to do something else, something far more difficult. You need to inquire into everything you see, honestly and soberly and without prejudice. And this is not as easy as it seems.

You can't deny it, we are certainly not on friendly terms with America now, or rather with the United States. We two nations are the largest and most powerful in the world, and we are ideological and political enemies. Twenty years ago we were allies, but now we are enemies. A terrible word. You don't even want to say it, and maybe you shouldn't say it. Still, it's no use pretending. We do not trust each other, we are wary of each other, and we accuse each other.

Under these conditions, it is not easy to travel around the country, much less write about it. And it's not easy to communicate with people. But communication is the most important thing, with friends or enemies. Only through communication with people can you find what you are looking for, in any depth at all. And the most interesting things are life and what people live by. The Empire State and the Chrysler buildings come afterward.

What Ivan Ivanovich was most afraid of was any deviation from our daily schedule. He was always in a state of tension and anxiety, constantly counting us like chickens, and the worst thing that could happen to him was for someone to say: "I don't want to go to the Metropolitan, I want to go to the Guggenheim, or maybe just take a little walk on Broadway." For some reason he dreaded this "little walk" the most of all.

On our first day in New York, he set up the first team conference, the first "briefing session," at the entrance to the United Nations Building. He asked Tadeusz Osipowicz to step aside for a moment and gave us a little speech about discipline, about the problems and duties of a Soviet collective on foreign soil, about how so and so had been late for dinner on the very first day and got separated from the collective, so that he had to take a taxi. He said this must not happen again, otherwise he would be required to take the appropriate steps. What they were, he didn't say. Like school children, we stood along the wall of the famous building, listening to him in silence. And then we defendants began to justify ourselves. Voices gradually rose, and an argument started. Tadeusz Osipowicz, standing off to one side, looked at us ironically. It was rather shameful.

Poor, poor Ivan Ivanovich. In a way, I understood him. I was even a little sorry for him. After all, he was responsible for all of us, twenty people he didn't know and who had only known each other for about twenty-four hours. And we were not at home, but in the City of the Yellow Devil * with its gangsters, police, and F.B.I. How could you fail to sympathize with him? But our kind Ivan Ivanovich forgot one thing: the local citizens were drawn to us Soviet people, they were anxious to talk to us, and we had no right to turn away from them and keep to ourselves. They watched everything we did and listened to everything we said, and so we had to act completely naturally. We had to be our-

* What Gorky called New York in his travel book *In America*. (*Translator's note*)

selves. Excessive caution—let us call it that—does not bring people together. It drives them apart.

Anyway, despite all the regulations and the strict time-table, we managed to learn something about America. Not a great deal, but something anyway.

And so (I've gotten off the track), let's begin with New York. There's been so much written about it that I'm almost afraid to begin. We were there five days, hardly any time at all. But strange as it may seem, it doesn't take long to get used to this Babylon. At first the skyscrapers are astonishing, especially the ones in Manhattan. But after a while you feel as though you've been seeing them all your life, walking around among them, taking trips to the hundredth floor. It's absolute nonsense to say they are depressing. (Hitler's Imperial Chancellery in Berlin is a much smaller building, but I find it much more depressing.) Some of them, those built in recent years, are light (actually light!), airy, and transparent. There is a great deal of glass in them, and they reflect each other in an amusing way. In the morning and evening when the sun strikes them at an angle and lights them up, they are simply beautiful. Next to them the skyscrapers built at the turn of the century seem archaic: a Greek portico on the thirtieth floor only makes you smile.

At the top of the Empire State, the tallest building in the world, there is an observation deck. For a certain sum of money, you can ride up there in one of two swift elevators, look at the city through a telescope, have a cup of coffee, and buy souvenirs.

And, of course, we all rode up there. I must say that when you stand there above this city with the dozens of sky-scrapers clustered together in the enormous space below you, with the little cars and tiny creatures crawling in the canyons among them, and beyond, the East River, the Brooklyn Bridge and the Hudson, with its docks and ships, when you stand up there with the wind in your face and look down at this giant city or octopus city—whatever you want to call it—you can't help feeling excited. I had a similar feeling once when I was on the peak of Mount Elbrus. Beneath me stretched the Caucasus. Everything lay below me. Even Mount Kazbek. There I was struck by the grandeur and beauty of nature around me, but here I was struck by the grandeur and beauty of man. Everything here was created by him, by his hands and his brain. . . .

And then you have to ask yourself a question. How many Empire State Buildings and Chrysler Buildings and bridges like the swift, airy George Washington Bridge across the Hudson, how many useful things could be built with the money that is being spent on all those Polarises, Honest Johns, and other merry playthings of the twentieth century? (By the way, full-scale models of missiles stand in front of the various military institutions in America, just as the old cannons stood there in their time, and we even saw one of these missiles in the concourse of Grand Central Station. What is it doing there?)

New York is not young any longer. (In its early youth, when it was held by the Dutch, it was called New Amsterdam and New Orange.) It is already three hundred years old. Legend has it that the Dutch seafarer, Peter Minuit, bought Manhattan Island from the Iroquois Indians for twenty-four dollars.

For five years New York was the capital of the nation, from 1785 to 1790. Now it is the capital of only one state. With its eight million people, it has spread out over three islands and one peninsula. It is divided into five parts,

Brooklyn, Queens, the Bronx, Richmond, and Manhattan, a narrow island which has everything crowded onto it. In turn, Manhattan is divided into three parts: *Downtown,* from the southern tip of the island to Twenty-third Street; *Midtown,* from Twenty-third Street to Central Park at Fifty-ninth Street; and *Uptown,* from Fifty-ninth Street to the northern end. *Midtown* is the smallest part but the most famous: it has the U.N. Building, Rockefeller Center, two great railroad stations, Pennsylvania and Grand Central, two great skyscrapers, the Empire State and the Chrysler Building, and finally the hub of New York, Times Square. Nearby, not far from Broadway, is where we lived in our hotel, the Governor Clinton, an enormous stone affair of twenty-eight stories: "Excellently located in the center of Manhattan, with 1,200 rooms, air-conditioning, twenty-one-inch television (some rooms have color TV), convenient, comfortable, and friendly."

Manhattan is marked out like a checkerboard. Up and down the length of the island run fourteen avenues and two highways along the shore. And from east to west, at right angles to the avenues, there are two hundred and twenty streets. (Our hotel was located on the corner of Seventh Avenue and Thirty-first Street.) And across the whole island, breaking the regularity of the checkerwork, runs Broadway—swift and oblique—probably the longest street in the world, about twelve miles long.

The first morning, we rushed out onto it. The real Broadway, the heart of New York, is really a small strip from Thirty-fourth to Fifty-second Street. (One of our Kievans compared it to our Kreshchatik.) This is the part that shows up in all the movies about New York, New York as everybody imagines it, the city of light and entertainment, especially this part. This is Times Square, the famous

"Crossroads of the World" (the intersection of Broadway, Forty-second Street and Seventh Avenue). This is where everyone has his picture taken with the Chevrolet advertisement as a backdrop (even we couldn't resist), or the fascinating young smoker, two stories high and famous throughout the world, who blows out enormous rings of real smoke, bringing fame to Camel cigarettes.

In other words, for all its length, Broadway is really a very small street. And what is really strange about it is that it begins to thin out after eleven o'clock at night, just when the evening is beginning on the Kreshchatik of Rome, the Via Veneto. Once I walked home on Broadway late at night, and it was strange to see this whirl of light, blinking, glittering, all for me. Broadway was empty.

Another thing that surprised me was all the little shops, like cracks in the wall. In some of them you see teenagers, old men, and even old women, playing some kind of electric games which I couldn't understand. Others have all kinds of amusing trinkets for sale, wriggling snakes that look almost real, shrunken Indian heads with long hair (don't worry—they're only plastic), horrible-looking masks, and all kinds of mechanical toys, jumping things, spinning things, squeaking things.

By the way, speaking of toys, in America they are wonderful. Once I stood for a long time in front of a model-railroad window (it happened to be in Brussels but the toys were American) and I couldn't tear myself away. There were three trains: a freight drawn by a diesel engine, a passenger with a steam engine, and an express with an electric one. The three of them made wide circles around an elaborate network of track. They ducked into tunnels and clattered over bridges, they stopped at stations and semaphores, whistled and shrieked, and they never once

collided. Beyond, there was an airport with occasional air-
planes landing. And that's not all. As soon as it was evening, the lights came on in the windows of the houses, and
the headlights of the locomotives cast their beam along the
tracks. I had a hard time turning away from this spectacle.
I had spent my whole childhood dreaming of trains like
these, but I never had any. (Trains like these? They were
even beyond my dreams.) If I had the money now, I'd
certainly buy them. Not for myself, of course, but for the
eight-year-old son of a friend of mine. But before I gave
them to him, I'd take them into my room and lock the
door, so no one could see what I was doing.

The soldiers, too, are unbelievably intriguing. They
used to be called "tin soldiers," but I don't know what they
are made of now. There are soldiers of all types and sizes,
of all nationalities, and all periods of history. Americans,
Indians, Arabs, Napoleonic grenadiers, knights, and *Bersa-
glieri*. The only ones I didn't see were Red Army men.
And the costumes. They would keep any young person
awake at night. Take the cowboy suit for example: a hat
with a broad turned-down brim, fringed pants, a necker-
chief, and a pair of Colts in holsters on a broad belt with
luxurious metal ornaments. For the finishing touch, you
can buy a sheriff's star.

And I saw other toys just as cleverly made. For example,
the "Boeing Bomber" that actually flies and drops bombs.
Or a tank with a rocket launcher. You see it advertised on
television: the tank seems to be crawling toward you out of
the screen, it picks up speed, levels its cannon at you, and
then . . .

"For the best entertainment for your children, these are
the toys to buy!"

But back to Broadway. That strip between Thirty-fourth and Fifty-second streets has more movie houses and theaters than anything else. Unfortunately we didn't get to the theater, even though the Broadway theater is the most interesting and characteristic aspect of New York theatrical life. But we did go to the movies, on the very first day. We were attracted by advertisements for the famous Elvis Presley, the idol of American teenagers. This twenty-year-old youngster, good-looking, if a little saccharine, took America by storm with his songs a few years ago. If I'm not mistaken, the world is indebted to him for "rock and roll." In a few weeks, Presley became a millionaire. He became so popular that when it came time for him to be drafted into the army, the United States Defense Department received thousands of letters and telegrams from lovesick girls, pleading for their idol. But the Defense Department took him anyway. Elvis served his time in the army, and in doing so, he incidentally provided the subject matter for the film we saw: *Elvis in the Army.*

It was a trivial comedy, amusing at times. Elvis did no rock and roll. He didn't even sing very much, but when he did, it was pleasant enough. He spent most of the time sighing over a girl, and she did the same over him, and they kissed a few times, and that was it. This entertainment cost us a dollar each, and I can tell you confidentially, it was also partly responsible for that lecture we had to endure in the first briefing session in front of the U.N., especially three of us, the movie-goers.

We didn't go to the movies any more. But we got an idea of what American movies were like because in every one of our hotel rooms there were those twenty-one-inch television sets that operated twenty-two hours a day, on eleven channels. And the fighting! What fighting we saw! In bars, in the streets, on trains, in luxurious hotels. At sea, underground, in the air. Tables and chairs were turned over, the blood flowed in rivers, and so many shots were fired that a good two weeks after I got home, they were still ringing in my ears. The men leaped nimbly around the saloons, turning somersaults, crashing bodily through unopened doors, landing outside in the middle of the street. Then, pausing a moment to wipe off their noses, they would go back in again, and a minute later, their opponent would come flying out, through the window this time. The chasing, the jumping. I'd never seen anything like it since I was a child. And now, perhaps, the cars are even longer, lower, and faster. We saw Rasputin himself, and Russian princes in troikas, and a hypnotist, and voluptuous women dangling Tarzan-like men at their finger tips. The only trouble was that right at the crucial moment a pretty girl would suddenly appear and for a long time we would have to watch her washing her hair with a special new kind of shampoo. Or else a charming couple would sit down together on the banks of a scenic lake and couldn't kiss each other until the young man had heard of the latest pill for bad breath. Every ten minutes the film is interrupted for little vignettes like these. Every program means advertising, and the television station exists on the proceeds of the advertising. And just imagine, the advertising actually works. It even worked on us. By the end of our trip, every single one of us had bought the magic "Anacin" tablets to relieve headaches. I bought them, too, despite the fact that I don't ever seem to get headaches.

Yes, American television is a frightening phenomenon. I had heard a great deal about it, but I had to see it to understand. Really, how can you avoid killing off your neighbor, how can you help dealing him the "knock-out" blow, when from morning till night the television does nothing but show you better ways to do it? You'd better do it to him, or else he'll do it to you.

They talked about this a lot at the writers' congress in Florence. There is even a new term for it: *demiculture,* or *mass media* as the English call it, or *mass culture* in America. It includes most Western movies, comic books, pulp fiction, and picture magazines, anything to help you break the habit of thinking. Television is one of the best ways, of course, because immediately it does away with books and conversation.

By the way, television is the curse not only of America. In the Soviet Union we don't have brawling and street fighting or TV wrestling, the most monstrous of all sports (if such a bestial sort of torture can be called a sport at all). But we are cursed with something else: we wear out our viewing audience with endless interviews and amateur hours, until they languish in the depths of boredom. Maybe you have to have these programs so that the studio can fulfill its plan, but the trouble is that the audience can't endure to watch them any more. And just look at the audience itself: a whole family sitting around the table, staring at the television set. The theater, the movies, books, and guests, everything is forgotten. And the eyes gaze on, at the flickering screen.

No, I consider television only a means of reporting. To show you Gagarin stepping out of his spaceship onto the red carpet, the reception in Moscow for Titov, Nikolayev, and Popovich; to take you in person to the festival at Helsinki; to let you hear what Jean Paul Sartre has to say. At the very most, it can give you another chance at a film you have missed.

America's second curse is the broad, dark stream of detective literature. Really it could fill a whole sea. A lot has been written about these books, the ones that have a pistol pointing at you from the front cover. So much has been written that I'm almost ashamed to write any more, but I can't ignore them. I don't want to say anything derogatory about American bookstores: there are many of them and they sell a lot of interesting, serious books. But good books cost money, and all that detective poison hardly costs anything at all: it gets into you before you even realize it. The worst part is that people actually thirst for it: they drink it down eagerly. Especially young people.

I'm very sorry for the American boy. In general, he is a good, straightforward, kindly sort of person. But I pitied him when I saw him sitting in the subway with an athletic bag on his knees, reading a pulp novel that he'd just bought at a newstand for twenty-five cents: tomorrow he would throw it away in one of those huge baskets for old newspapers which stand on every street corner in New York. My God, I pitied him. Of course, you don't have to read Faulkner in the subway on your way to a workout or a ball game, but frankly, I'm afraid this youngster doesn't read Faulkner at home either.

Let me run ahead a little, to the end of our trip. We were riding from Buffalo to New York. We had a separate coach to ourselves: an aisle in the middle and two rows of seats on either side. We were all a little tired out by what we had seen and were gazing lazily through the wide, plate-glass windows. Outside, "Little Golden America" was flickering by. Some people had fallen asleep. My head was nodding, too.

Then suddenly the car door opened, and two boys poked their heads inside. They looked us over, and then one of them produced some broken Russian:

"You're Russians, aren't you?"

"Yes, we are."

"May we talk to you?"

"You may."

"We'll be right back."

Instantly, they disappeared, and a minute later the car was full of young people. They were all "upperclassmen," as we would say, youngsters about sixteen years old, on a trip to New York for a few days. There was a teacher in charge of them, a middle-aged man, who was no less worried than our Ivan Ivanovich by this sudden confrontation of the two worlds.

The boys were talkative and curious. Immediately we got farther than the usual exchange of pins, post cards, and coins. Two or three of them were studying Russian, and one way or another we managed to communicate.

I liked these youngsters. They behaved freely and naturally, and you could sense a certain intelligence in what they asked about and what they said. I realized that perhaps not now, but in a few years, they would be reading Faulkner. The conversation jumped around. We talked about Moscow, New York, about our jackets, about war, baseball, movies (some of them had seen *Ballad of a Soldier* and had liked it very much) and about plans for the future. On this last question they talked rather vaguely, or sometimes facetiously: "First, I'll open a business, and then I'll try to take over from Kennedy." (Kennedy had just been elected President the week before.) Generally, Americans are fond of humor and they appreciate it, but I was struck by this "First I'll open a business," even if it was said in fun. We didn't have a particularly meaningful exchange on this subject, and after singing a round of "Moscow Nights" and an American favorite we brought our meeting to a close.

In New York we parted, and in a jolly group, swinging their suitcases, they disappeared into the crowd. At this point, of course, it is hard to say which one of them will take over from Kennedy, but unfortunately it is true that at least a quarter of them will try to "open a business."

The question of young people is an eternal one. In all latitudes, fathers sigh the same lament: "We were never that way. . . ." I read somewhere that they found a papyrus in Egypt written six thousand years ago, in which a pharaoh complained about young people. Young people, he said, are becoming lazy and disrespectful. They don't want to work, and they prefer to spend their time writing. Well, the pharaoh was certainly farsighted, you can't deny that. But seriously, as far as young people are concerned, we must admit that the problem now is even more difficult, if possible, than it was in ancient Egypt.

We look at the Soviet young people of today, and sometimes we admire what we see, and sometimes we can only shake our heads. Certainly there are some first-rate students and some good-for-nothings as well; there are bookworms and *stilyagi,* crusaders and careerists, youngsters in spectacles and youngsters with black eyes. But that's not the question. The question is really much more serious. It's a question of one's philosophy of life, the search for one's place in the world. There are some very serious young people, and work and study means everything to them. But there are also some among them who might say: "I know my job and I like it, and that's all I care about." For these young people, you can see, work and study have become blinders. And there is also another variety, a more complicated one. Take the physicist for example: he's a good physicist; he's also interested in Heinrich Boell; * he goes

* Contemporary German novelist. (*Translator's note*)

to Richter concerts and the Mexican Exhibition. But God save him from politics. "That's a shady business," he says. There are even more complex, more serious young people, the ones who torment themselves with anything to do with the cult of personality. These are the ones who say, "We want to know the truth," and these are the ones who will have the hardest time of all.

But whatever these youngsters are like (and I don't mean the bottom of the barrel that you're bound to have anywhere), their personal aspirations, their plans for a career, are not usually directed to their own advantage. There is also such a thing as duty: duty to the people, to the country, one's duty to oneself. I think that's the main thing that separates our young people from the young people of the bourgeois West. It's not the fact that ours spend their evenings at Komsomol meetings, while they spend theirs in black sweaters and tight pants, doing the rock and roll and the twist.

I had an argument about this in a little cottage near Washington. I had gone there at the invitation of the Veteran's Friendship Society. We were invited by a tall, pleasant-looking young fellow who spoke Russian fairly well. He came to our hotel just when we were having dinner, and presented us with calling cards with a symbol of clasped hands etched on them. He told us that the members of this society would be very happy to have us come over to their homes in groups of two and three. As usual in cases like this, Ivan Ivanovich immediately lost his head: you see, these visits were not included on the schedule. But the young man was so disappointed—"Are you really more interested in museums and skyscrapers than you are in people?"—that it was impossible to refuse.

I don't remember who owned the house I went to. I went

there with a lady who drove the car very aggressively. As far as I could make out, she was the daughter of a Russian emigré.

"Just call me Olga," she said.

When we got there, we found a cozy little cottage and a group of ten people or so, including two Russians: Olga's husband, Leo Nikolayevich, who was a quiet, middle-aged journalist, and Volodya, a very lively young man about twenty years old. Volodya and I got into a discussion that was only over at three or four in the morning in our Washington hotel room.

At first everything was very pleasant. Everybody was talking, drinking wine and cognac, then coffee by candlelight. The hostess had prepared everything very comfortably and tastefully. But by twelve o'clock or so, Volodya began to warm up, and he brought the conversation around to the important questions.

At that point, Olga said, "Why don't we go over to my house now? You can finish your argument there. These American people aren't interested in it anyway, and at the same time you can see my children."

And so we went to her house. We had some more coffee, and we saw her children, two adorable, golden-haired little boys, who remained fast asleep. And we continued our argument. Volodya was an intelligent fellow, vigorous and sincere. He was born in America and he had never been to Russia, but he criticized our system and extolled the American way of life.

When you argue like this with people who are obviously not sympathetic to our system, the questions usually run like this: "Why do you have only one party? Why have you forbidden abstractionism? Why can't you buy the New

York *Times* on the streets of Moscow? Why do you jam the Voice of America? Where is your freedom?"

And then we answer: "Why do you persecute the Communist party? Why did you deport Charlie Chaplin? Why do you have military bases all over the world? Why are you trying to strangle Cuba? Why do you let your generals make inflammatory speeches? Is that what you mean by freedom?"

There is not much point in exchanges like these. They only make for bitterness on both sides. It's much more important to learn something about the psychology of your opponent (assuming, of course, he's a worthy opponent), and then get through to the heart of the question (assuming, of course, the question is a serious one). Then, without boasting and without trying to prove that your system is better in every way than your opponent's, you can quietly and clearly demonstrate the justice of your point of view.

It's hard for me to judge how convincing I really was that night, but arguing with Volodya about youth and the direction it is taking, I think I had some success.

I don't mean to idealize all our Soviet youngsters who go out to the construction projects. Not all of them go for idealistic reasons, far from it. But a good many of them do go because they believe they are needed there and because they are doing the country some good. Is such a thing possible in America? I doubt it. The young American, even the searching and thinking American, is concerned first of all with himself, with his career. For example, it is hard to imagine one of our young men saying: "I want this because it will be to my advantage." This would simply be considered improper. Even if he thought so, he would not say it out loud; he would simply be ashamed to. But the young American considers this completely normal. It is not his fault by any means. It is demanded by the iron laws of his society.

My argument with Volodya was over early in the morning. As he said good-by he said to me: "I concede. I never thought it would turn out this way, but I concede."

I never saw him again because we left the next day. But I'd be very interested to know just what effect our nocturnal dialogue really had on his views of our country and our people. Even though he doesn't know it, they are a country and a people that can't help but be dear to him. And it seems to me that his very eagerness to argue is a part of the whole conflict within himself, his need to reconcile himself with the fact that he is so far away from the great events that have taken place in the land of his fathers.

Volodya, of course, is not typical. He is too much of a Russian in his taste for argument and for proving his point. The American is not that interested in arguing. Essentially, the average American—the rank-and-file American, as he is called nowadays (factory worker, office employee, or student)—is not very inclined to analyzing and philosophizing. This is not primitivism, as some people have called it, and not intellectual laziness either. Rather I would call it a kind of infantilism. (The American even looks younger than he really is.) As a cheerful student at Columbia University told me once: "We don't like them to stuff us full of a lot of trash." Here, of course, you have to define what you mean by trash, but let me repeat, in contrast to the Italian, the American doesn't like to argue. He prefers a friendly chat over a glass of something strong. He likes a good joke, a prank or two, a good time. By nature he is very friendly and trusting, very simple and natural in his relationships. If you go to his house, he wants everything to be simple and cheerful. He doesn't like boredom, and he doesn't like protocol or formality.

I remember the dark cloud of boredom that settled over our good hosts in Buffalo, when after the second glass of cognac, one of our tourists (a university professor) pulled out his notebook and began to recite the latest figures on steel, pig iron, manganese, and coal production in the Ukraine. And I also remember how, on the other hand, everyone was delighted with another one of our tourists (a young Moscow newspaperman) who won everyone over with the very first thing he told the host.

"I see you have a 1960 Ford in your garage," he said. "Can I take it out for a spin at 100 miles an hour?"

He did take his spin, and afterward he poked around under the hood with our host; he got into an argument with someone about a baseball game the day before; and he challenged someone else to a wrestling match. The Americans wouldn't leave him alone. But our poor professor sat in the corner with his figures in his pocket: everyone had forgotten him.

Yes, first of all, you must be yourself, and only afterward a preacher. Besides, isn't that the best sermon of all, to be yourself?

When I'd written down all these thoughts and this manuscript was almost finished, I happened to see a film in Moscow which brought me back again to the subject of young people. I'm referring to Marlen Khutsiyev's *Guard of Lenin*.

I am not afraid of exaggerating when I say that this film is a great event in the history of our art, a very great event. I saw it with Andrzej Wajda, author of the film *Ashes and*

Diamonds, and a man whom you can unquestionably place among the first ten directors in the world. After it was over, he said straightaway that he had never seen a film quite like it. (And I think Wajda has seen a fair number of films in his day.) He said he could go right back in and see it again. And you must remember, the film does last for two hours and forty-five minutes.

Let me repeat, I don't doubt for a moment that this film has become a landmark in our cinematic art: in its ideas, its direction, its photography. (Marguerita Pilikhina has shown us a Moscow which we've never seen on the screen before, a real Moscow, a Moscow you couldn't invent, so poetic that sometimes the tears come to your eyes from the sheer joy of recognition.) The acting is free of every strain (and these young people have never been in films before). The dialogue is light and free and vibrant with life. (Khutsiyev wrote the scenario with Genady Shpalikov.) For me, even though I have some complaints about the direction, all this is true, great art—art that is sincere, true to life, honest.

A lot has been written about young people, and a lot of films made about them, both here and abroad, but I've never read any book or seen any film that dramatizes the question of young people as keenly or with such personal involvement as this film.

Everyone has seen the fine American film *Marty,* but not everyone has seen *Love at Twenty,* which consists of five sketches done by five different directors, a Frenchman, an Italian, a German, a Japanese, and a Pole. Both films are about young people. In the second film, two of the sketches are especially good: the first, by the Frenchman Truffaut (the same two boys are in it who were in the *400 Blows,* only they're grown up now, twenty years old); and the last

114

one, by Andrzej Wajda—but let me get to him another time, not in this essay. The remaining three are considerably weaker, though each one of them has its own particular authenticity, its own truth.

Why do I remember these two films, *Marty* and *Love at Twenty?* Because together with Khutsiyev's film they give you an interesting and authentic picture of the way of life of our contemporary twenty-year-olds, in different countries and on different continents.

In Truffaut's film, the hero falls in love very tenderly and purely, but finally nothing comes of it. For the hero from West-Germany, the whole problem is in the fact that the girl he loves bears him a son (he's a successful journalist, she a telephone operator). In the Italian sketch (it was directed by Rosselini's son) a young man is torn between two mistresses, one rich and one poor. The Japanese story ends with the hero's murdering the heroine. And finally, to return to America, we learn something about the life of that charming young American Marty, and we witness his first, timid love.

Different countries, different youngsters. The Parisian works in a company that makes phonograph records; the German is a journalist; you don't know what the Italian does; the Japanese is a worker; Marty owns a butchershop in New York; Khutsiyev's youngsters are all workers. They are all about twenty, not much more than that. And, of course, they are all in love, each one in his own way. They all have their gay moments, and their sadder ones. (Except for the Japanese boy, who is always haunted. In general, this film doesn't fit into the over-all plan.) And they have their moments of boredom, too. (In *Marty* and *Guard of Lenin,* you hear the same thing: "Where shall we go, boys? What shall we do tonight?") But only in one film, in

Khutsiyev's, do the youngsters ask themselves, "Well, and after that, then where are we?"

The heroes of *Guard of Lenin* are all close friends. They have a good time together. They all have a fairly good life, nothing exceptional, but no exceptional hardship either. They do their work, one in a factory, one with a computer company, the third on a construction project. They meet in the evenings, they go out together, and have a few drinks: in other words, they're friends. But complications are bound to arise in this life, and ruffle its even surface. Slavka has a wife and child, but sometimes he just likes to hang around with the boys: his wife is cramping his style. Kolka has trouble with his boss: once he almost hauled off and hit him in the face. Sergey has suddenly fallen in love with the daughter of an important comrade, and the old man is an unpleasant brute. Questions come up, as they have to: "What do we do now? What is the right thing? How can you be sure it's right? How are you supposed to live anyway?"

I am endlessly grateful to Khutsiyev and Shpalikov for not dragging in the old worker by his graying mustache, the one who understands everything and always has exactly the right answer for anything you ask him. If he had come by with his instructive sayings, it would have ruined the picture. Instead, they tried something else, something much more difficult. Sergey takes the question to his father, his father who died at the front: he asks his father how he should live. This is one of the most powerful scenes in the movie. A meeting of father and son. Is it a dream, a fantasy, a hallucination? I don't know. But the son meets his father. His father is wearing his army cap and poncho, and he is carrying a machine gun across his chest. Suddenly the room is transformed into a dugout. Soldiers are lying asleep where they have fallen. On the table there is a lamp made out of a shell case. Father and son have a drink together.

The son tells the father, "I wish I'd been with you in the attack, when you were killed."

"Why," says the father. "You must live."

And the son asks, "But how?"

And the father only asks a question in return: "How old are you now?"

"Twenty-three."

"And I am only twenty-one."

These last words make the shivers run up and down your spine.

The father leaves without answering the question. His comrades are waiting for him. And they set off, three soldiers in ponchos, three comrades with machine guns across their chests, marching through the Moscow of today. A car speeds past them, but they don't turn around. They march on just as, at the beginning of the picture, three other soldiers marched along the streets of another Moscow, a Moscow of 1917, three soldiers of the Revolution. And the even staccato of their footsteps is drowned out by other footsteps: Red Square, the changing of the guard, the Mausoleum, and the inscription: Lenin.

There are many other levels of meaning, other turning points, other encounters, and complexities, but it all comes down to the same question, "Well, after that, then where are we?"

There is one answer, just as there always is. The constant search for answers, the search for the right thing to do, the search for the truth. As long as you are searching, asking questions, asking yourself, your friends, your father, asking your questions on Red Square, you are alive. When there are no more questions, there is no more you. A prosperous, untroubled, satisfied existence, a life without questions, is no life at all.

This has turned out something like a movie review. A very sketchy one, perhaps, but a review just the same. I didn't mean it to. I wanted to do something else. I wanted to make some statement about what our young people are like. I wanted to answer the question, "After all, how are they different from Western youngsters?" Khutsiyev and Shpalikov have given the answer for me.

I don't doubt that there are youngsters like these in the West; there are bound to be. You can find them in Cuba, in America, in Italy, and in France. But this is the first time you can find them in our art. And that, I think, has a certain significance.

At nine thirty in the morning on the third day of our visit to America, we set out for Washington on a train called "The Executive."

In America, all trains have names. On the Pennsylvania Railroad, which mainly serves three states—Pennsylvania, Ohio, and Indiana—there are trains called "The President," "The General," "The Admiral," "The Golden Triangle," "The South Wind," "The Patriot," "The Edison," "The Legislator," "The Half Moon," "The Pilgrim," "The William Penn," "The Hellgate" and at least a dozen more.

Even since my childhood, I have had a passion for anything to do with railroads, trains, steam engines, semaphores, bridges, stations, even timetables. I still think of the steam engine as a living creature. When I was twelve years old, when we used to live near Kiev, I used to run down to the station a dozen times a day to see my beloved steam engines. Mostly, the NV and the NY engines used to pass through there, and sometimes the A and the B, and sometimes on the only mail train from Kiev to Kazatin there would be a good-looking C type, "The Prairie," sharp-nosed and proud, with a short smokestack and electric headlights. (All the others had kerosene lamps.) I knew them all by their character, their habits, and their voice. And if for some reason the evening mail train came without the C-513 but the B or the NY instead, I began to worry: Was my good friend sick this evening? Now the steam engine is no more. You don't even see the CY or its descendant the C, except occasionally on branch lines.

In America there are no steam engines at all. The impersonal electric engines and diesels have replaced them. But at the Henry Ford Museum in Dearborn, I was pleasantly surprised to meet an old friend (I had seen him before in illustrations of Jules Verne and the films of the twenties), the steam engine "Pacific": a wide smokestack, an enormous headlight, the inevitable bell in the engineer's cab and a cowcatcher ahead of the little cart in front. (By the way, we had a diesel on the train trip from Niagara to Buffalo, but it also had a bell, and for some unknown reason it kept ringing the whole trip.) In the museum, I spent most of my time in the steam-engine section. It has all the American trains that Henry Ford collected, all the way from the old Stevensonian rockets with cars no bigger than mail coaches and idyllic pictures on the walls and doors, to the powerful titans with wheels twice as high as a man. Now they stand side by side—the pathetic, undersized grandfather, and the grandson beside him, frighteningly huge in comparison —and both of them are already in the past. . . . You can also see the famous train in which Thomas Edison sold newspapers as a boy, in which an officious conductor boxed his ears, so that he was deaf for his whole life afterward. In that train, which Henry Ford bought especially, Edison celebrated his eightieth birthday in a very original way: he walked up and down the aisles and sold newspapers again.

Present-day American trains are comfortable and convenient. They are made up of different types of cars, all very long. The cheapest way to travel is by *coach,* a car with an aisle in the middle and seats on either side; more expensive is the *sleeping car;* then there is an *observation car,* with two stories especially designed for people who like to look at the countryside, and finally there is a *lounge car,* a sort of *wagon-salon.* I never rode in a *lounge car,* but we did ride in a *sleeping car* from Washington to Chicago. Well, let us just say that our first-class accommodations are more comfortable. The American *sleeping car* has a very complicated arrangement of compartments on both sides of the aisle and on two levels, and to get into the top compartments you have to use a stepladder. But what surprised us most—and in fact it posed a crucial problem for us right away—was how to find the toilet. We looked for it all over the car, but it was nowhere. Finally, it turned up, right in the compartment itself. It seemed I had been sitting on it all the time.

New York to Washington is a four-hour trip. "The Executive" goes seventy miles an hour. Past Philadelphia, Wilmington, Baltimore. Past smaller American towns, with neat little white houses, each one like the other, standing out in contrast to the greenery around them. Past factories and warehouses. Past hundreds of cars speeding along on the highways beside us, to the southwest: to the capital of the nation, to Washington. Sometimes, we would stop for a moment at some place like New Brunswick or Trenton, take on some passengers and leave a few, and then hurry on again.

The passengers doze or leaf through magazines, which at the end of the trip will be scattered all over the car, like documents in an abandoned German headquarters during the war. I sit at a window and think back over my childhood.

I used to have a friend called Yasya. Together we published a newspaper of the future called the *Radio*, dated the year 1979. We put out about ten or twelve issues, but unfortunately the "files" are gone now: the Germans burned them along with the house we used to live in. More than thirty years have passed since then, and there are less than twenty years to go before 1979, but it's hard to keep from smiling when I think back over those days: reality has so eclipsed our childish dreams and fantasies. We were ahead of it in only one respect (and anyway there are still many years to go), in space travel: we had already flown to Mars. But on the sinful old Earth, everything stayed on the level of the twenties. We didn't even dig a subway. We solved the transportation problem in Kiev simply by increasing the number of trolley lines to a hundred, and we thought that was great progress. And we fought wars in the old-fashioned way, against a nation called the Anglo-Ams (the English and the Americans). I don't remember what we were fighting about, but I do remember the battles took place in Alaska and they read exactly like the battles of Verdun and Champagne, all the more so because we illustrated them with pictures clipped out of the old *Neva* magazine and the French *L'Illustration*.

After a while we got tired of the newspaper; we ran out of inspiration, and so we went on to build the "World-Wide Railroad" instead: Moscow-Vladivostok-New York-Paris-Moscow. We built a bridge over the Bering Straits; and across the Atlantic, which at that time Lindbergh still hadn't crossed, we ran the trains across on high-speed ocean-going ferries. And on large sheets of paper left over from the newspaper, we drew up the timetable for our railroad. We had mail trains, combined freight and passenger trains, expresses, and super-expresses. We made up the timetable according to all the conventions: stations with restaurants, we marked with a little knife and fork, and sleeping cars with little beds. But we never finished it. We covered Siberia, Alaska, Canada, and the United States as far as Chicago. But then the summer vacation began, and that meant boat rides on the Dnieper, and a lot of other things that were much more exciting.

Now, thirty-odd years later, sitting in "The Executive," I thought back over our unfinished business. A few days later when we got to Chicago, I bought a New York-Chicago timetable of the Baltimore & Ohio Railway, put it in an envelope, and sent it to my friend. He's not Yasya now, but Yakov Mikhailovich, a geologist, historian, and linguist; and despite a sturdy age, he hasn't lost his sense of humor. Maybe now he would suddenly be compelled to complete that important and necessary work that was interrupted thirty years ago. But alas, for unknown reasons, the parcel never reached its addressee. Apparently, at the customs station, humor isn't valued very highly.

According to the pamphlets, Washington is the most beautiful capital in the world. Well, I won't try to decide whether it is or not. I'm afraid the authors of the pamphlet exaggerated just a little. But you can't deny that the typical parts of Washington are really beautiful. Especially in the fall: when the foliage is flaming in all shades of yellow, orange, and red, and the maple leaves slowly spiral down the air, and the white marble palaces stand out against the background of the deep blue sky, and the friendly gray squirrels jump around the trees and the fresh green lawns.

Washington is the least American of all American cities. It has hardly any industry, its houses are low, and its boulevards are broad and green. It is a quiet, peaceful city of government officials and it goes to bed early. Washington is relatively young, about the same age as Leningrad. And if you had to compare it to other capitals, you might say, as the guidebooks do, that whereas Paris, Rome, and London are capitals through circumstance, Washington is a capital through intention, through the intention of its founders. That is true: Washington is a preconceived city. The only cities that are more completely preconceived are Canberra, the capital of Australia, and Brasilia, the youngest capital of all.

Washington is two regular nets, one placed on top of the other. One is a rectangular network of numbered and lettered streets (there is A Street, B Street, and so on down to Z). The other is a diagonal network of avenues named after all the states, Pennsylvania, Massachusetts, Virginia, Maryland, New York and so on. The center is the Capitol. Leading away from it, there is a wide strip of land along the Potomac River, enclosed between two avenues, the only ones that do not run diagonally away from the Capitol: Independence and Constitution Avenues. At the end of this strip, there is a mausoleum overlooking the Potomac: the Lincoln Memorial. Between it and the Capitol Building, closer to it, there is a stone obelisk over five hundred feet high: the Washington Monument. To the north of it, at the crossing of Pennsylvania and New York Avenues at the center of town, is the White House. And that's the plan of Washington, all in all a very simple layout. It was designed by the Frenchman Pierre Charles l'Enfant.

Washington is the least American of all American cities, but as everywhere in America, it has its superlatives. The lobby of the Washington Station (Union Station) is 750 by 130 feet, the largest enclosed area in the world. The National Gallery of Art is the largest marble building in the world. The Marine Corps Memorial, the largest bronze statue in the world, The Arlington Bridge is the biggest drawbridge in the world. The Washington Monument is the biggest stone obelisk, maybe the biggest masonry obelisk in the world. (*Masonry:* stone, masonic. George Washington was a mason.*) The Church of the Immaculate Conception is the largest Catholic Cathedral in the United States (and one of the seven largest in the world), and in its southern apse, it has the largest mosaic representation of Christ (the dimensions of the head are 8 by 5 feet, the span between the outstretched arms is 34 feet, and the stones are in four thousand different colors).

Anyway, there is no question about it, Washington is truly beautiful. I'm not very fond of eclecticism and the imitation of many different styles, but I must admit that the pink-white-and-gold marble of the "Greek" porticoes and the colonnades of the museums and buildings all immersed in the greenery of the parks around them make a striking impression. Especially at night, when the water in the illuminated fountains rises in arches of many different colors, and the dome of the Capitol Building and the Washington Monument seem to be glowing with their own inner light.

The Capitol Building is not the best in Washington. It is pompous and ornate, strictly adhering to the traditional forms of nineteenth-century parliamentary buildings. The

---

* A play on words. Nekrasov must have thought the English word *masonry* (rendered in English in the Russian text) was an adjective meaning both *stone* and *masonic*. Thus, the obelisk is a *masonic* monument (since George Washington himself was a mason). (*Translator's note*)

Washington Monument, on the other hand, is very concise in its geometrical simplicity: a marble needle thrust into the sky, worthy of the name it immortalizes. It took a long time to build it, a very long time: forty years, from 1848 to 1888. It is over five-hundred feet high, or more precisely, 555 feet, 5 and ⅛ inches. From the apex (there is a special place up there to which an elevator will take you in seventy seconds) you have a lovely view of the city and the surrounding countryside. We came down by an iron staircase, which is very hard work, but that way we could touch all the stones which went into its long construction (it was delayed by the Civil War). Among them there are enormous blocks with inscriptions by different people, associations, cities, states, and even nations. There are also some stones that are the only ones of their kind: pieces of the Parthenon and Carthage, Napoleon's tombstone from St. Helena, and a stone from the chapel of William Tell in Switzerland. Perhaps this is the most moving part of the whole monument.

Not far from the obelisk there is a monument to another of America's sons: the Lincoln Memorial. In a way, it's a paraphrase of the Parthenon in Athens, austere, blindingly white, all hewn out of Colorado marble. It is not a tomb, but rather a temple, built in honor of the great President. In the midst of it sits Lincoln himself, carved in marble, pensive and serious, tired and a little sad: he sits in a marble armchair, his right foot a little ahead of the other and his large beautiful hands resting on the arms of the chair. I don't recognize the name of the sculptor—Daniel Chester French—but I can say with confidence that for the psychological penetration of the artist into the character of the man he is attempting to portray, I don't know anything to compare to it in our contemporary gal-

lery of official art. It's a striking combination of wisdom
and serenity, power and tragedy. Sitting before you in the
shadowy light of the chilly marble hall, a great man seems
to be looking ahead not only to his own tragic end, but
over the whole complex and contradictory fate of a people
to whom he has devoted his life. And as you look at his
pensive, wistful face, you can't help asking yourself a question that is especially melancholy for us Russians. Could
Abraham Lincoln have foreseen, could this fighter for truth
and justice have imagined what would happen in only half
a century, that some of his descendants, the descendants of
Washington and Jefferson, would try to smother the young
Soviet Republic just born on the other side of the world?

I've mentioned the name of Jefferson, the third President of the United States, a name greatly honored by Americans. Thomas Jefferson was an outstanding American edu-
cator, author of the Declaration of Independence, a friend
of Condorcet and Cabanis, a pupil of Jean Jacques Rous-
seau. He was, if you can put it that way, the most revolu-
tionary of American presidents. He welcomed the French
Revolution and worked to support it. It was his idea that
a revolution develops only to the extent that the mass of
people acquires education and an awareness of its political
rights. He fought hard against the narrow-mindedness of
the American Revolution of the eighteenth century, which
did not abolish slavery, did not solve the agrarian question
in the interests of the people, and did not give the people
genuine political rights. In this way, he heralded the need
for further revolutions in the United States. The Jeffer-
sonian tradition is being carried on today by the progressive forces in America in a struggle for true freedom and
democracy.

His memorial, the Thomas Jefferson Memorial, is a

round colonnade with a dome on top, standing beside a pretty little lake. They say it is especially beautiful in springtime when a pink sea of flowering cherry trees swirls around it, a gift to the city of Washington from the city of Tokyo in 1912.

Washington is quiet and peaceful; it goes to bed early. In the thoughtful waters of its lakes, the monuments contemplate their own past glory, and the squirrels jump on the lawns. The enormous halls of the National Gallery are hung with the priceless canvases of Giotto, Raphael, Holbein, Vermeer, Rembrandt, Constable, Renoir, Degas, and Manet. In the Smithsonian Institute, one of the most interesting museums in America, the full-dress uniforms of George Washington and General Grant are hung behind glass; the Wright Brothers' plane is carefully preserved, and the Spirit of St. Louis, which Charles Lindbergh flew across the ocean on May 20 and 21, 1927, in thirty-three and a half hours.

And in the Wax Museum, a museum of wax figures, you can have your picture taken sitting between Franklin and Jefferson at an exact replica of the table where the Declaration of Independence was signed, then later see your picture in the Washington *Observer*. In short, there is a fair amount to see in Washington.

We strolled along the elegant fence around the White House, beautiful and calm among the shadows of the ancient linden trees and elms. On the next day, on November 8, we would know who was next going to occupy that house, Nixon or Kennedy. According to the Constitution, the citizens of Washington may not vote in elections, but they may listen to the radio and watch television. That evening we watched television too and listened to Kennedy and Nixon.

Two young, energetic millionaires. Which one of them would win? Either way, how would the world be changed? In New York we saw hundreds of posters and photographs of the two smiling candidates, enormous banners hung across Broadway, urging you to vote for one candidate or the other, and at every street corner there were young people with clear, ringing voices starting up discussions and passing out leaflets. On the corner of Broadway and Forty-second Street, we even saw Henry Cabot Lodge, the Republican vice-presidential candidate; he was driving along in a car that was covered with flags and he was shouting through a megaphone.

This contest between two powerful capitalists made little difference to us Soviet people. Wasn't it all the same whoever won? One was supported by certain powerful trusts and monopolies, and the other was supported by others. But this struggle, a struggle between the Elephant and the Donkey (symbols of two rival parties, the Democratic and the Republican), actually costs millions of dollars. Most of the time it seemed funny and naïve to us. But Americans have a different opinion. The people we met of the left wing were definitely for Kennedy.

"You see, he is younger," they said. "There's never been such a young President, forty-two years old! He's more progressive. He has a good war record. . . . And—well, I suppose it must be hard for you people to figure out our domestic politics. But don't worry, we know who to vote for."

And so on the evening of November 9, we sat in front of the television like all Americans and watched them count up the votes, and we also "rooted" for Kennedy.

How long has it been since that day? How much has changed in the world in that time? But the same tension still exists between our country and the United States. In

New York, thousands of people wait in line for tickets for the Bolshoi Ballet, the Moiseyev Ensemble gets standing ovations. In Moscow, it's impossible to get tickets for Van Cliburn; *Moby Dick* with Rockwell Kent's illustrations is sold out in one day. But in the United Nations or in Geneva we still can make no progress.*

I remember a picture in an American magazine in the early days of the war. It showed Uncle Sam reaching across the sea to shake hands with Ivan, a blond young man in a Russian shirt. The caption read: "Our friendship is the foundation of peace." This is what they were writing in 1945. Shouldn't it still be true?

In the southern part of Arlington Cemetery, six American servicemen, cast in bronze and standing on a pedestal of polished labradorite, are raising the stars and stripes on the peak of Mount Suribachi on Iwo Jima. The scene actually took place on February 23, 1945, on a remote island in the Pacific; and now, cast in bronze, it stands as a tribute to the valor of the American Marine Corps. Three of the men died on that very island. A fourth, an Indian named Ira Hayes, died in 1955 and is buried not far from the monument. The remaining two are still living, and they can come to Arlington at any time to admire themselves in bronze.

You don't have to like this monument. It is very dynamic and as realistic as a photograph (they say that Weldon, the sculptor, actually used photographs while he was working on it). But when you look at this monument, it gives you something to think about. Six courageous young boys in helmets are raising the flag on the top of a mountain which,

* This book, of course, was written before the 1963 Test Ban Treaty. (*Translator's note*)

until then, they never knew existed. What brought them there? Why have three of them given their lives there and been buried there in alien soil?

The whole world knows the contribution America made to the war against fascism. The name of Franklin Roosevelt is revered all over the world. It's true that America has never known the horrors of an occupation, of bombardments and annihilation, but all the same, American soldiers have died in Pearl Harbor and the Philippines, in the Persian Gulf and the Solomon Islands, at Monte Cassino and the Himalayas. Three hundred thousand young Americans will never come home again. Americans have known not only the joys of victory, but the bitterness of defeat, at Pearl Harbor, in the tragedies of Corregidor and Bataan, in those terrifying days in the beginning of 1942, when it seemed that the Japanese would soon be in Australia and on the shores of America itself. Those days were much harder for us, of course, and we don't need to play down our own war record. But we Russians will never forget the help that was given us in those difficult days—the Sherman tanks, the Aero-Cobras, the Studebakers, the canned pork, and all the things we didn't see at the front, but which went into our industry.

You remember all this when you look at the monument to the six American soldiers. They fought against fascism just as we did. They fought far from their native land, and they knew all the time that their home was just as peaceful as it had always been. Three of them died there. And why did they die? So that arm bands with swastikas could appear again on young American sleeves, so that portraits of Hitler could hang in the headquarters of the neo-Nazi Birchers, so that the familiar *"Sieg Heil!"* could resound again? I know that these organizations have a very small following.

131

The majority of Americans feel only contempt and revulsion for them. But they exist just the same, and it's hard not to think of them when you stand by the monument to those six men who fought against fascism, which bore more hatred for mankind than anything else on earth.

Two weeks in American Express tourist buses.

"Ladies and gentlemen, hurry up please. We still have two museums to go, the aquarium, and a visit to the Chicago *Sun*."

We hurry into the bus, take our seats, and ride off to the museum, to the aquarium, and the newspaper offices. Everything is getting muddled in our memory. What did we do after that? What did we see? What did we miss? What substitutions did we make? What do we have left to do?

"Ladies and gentlemen, be up at eight, breakfast at nine. At nine thirty the Ford Plant, then Greenfield Village, and the Ford Museum, Edison's laboratory and the Wright Brothers' workshop. At five o'clock we leave for Detroit, then to Buffalo, and a bus to Niagara Falls."

It's like a movie. The Ford conveyor belts are flickering by, the workers' nimble fingers hover over them, picking up new parts for automobile bodies. The little 1920 Fords with brass horns. Edison's favorite armchair. Chemical flasks, test tubes, photographs, coal lamps, workbenches, vises.

"The very same ones which . . ."

Studios, print shops, a blacksmith's shop . . .

"The very same one which . . ."

My mind is spinning now.

"Ladies and gentlemen, up at eight, breakfast at nine . . ."

Museums, museums, museums. Oh, for God's sake, let's see some people! Let's see how they live, what they do with themselves, what they think about. . . .

That same Kiev newspaperman—let's call him K.—the member of our tourist group who was afraid he wouldn't have anything to write about because they hadn't shown him the slums, gave a series of lectures just as soon as he got home. There were posters all over town announcing, "America, November, 1960." I went to one of these lectures and heard him deal very thoroughly with slums, unemployment, poverty, the New York streets that never see the light of day, low wages and high rents, hard labor conditions, and strikes. Someone asked him about the prices of goods. He replied that he hadn't looked into this. A murmur ran through the audience. A young man timidly asked about alcoholism in America; did they drink much there?

"A great deal," K. replied. "In Washington—no, I'm sorry, in Chicago—we saw one drunk who could hardly stand up."

The audience burst out laughing. I was ashamed, even though I knew, thank God, you don't meet people like K. all the time.

Another of our Soviet journalists, one who had lived in New York for four years, told me once:

"America is really a land of contrasts, very striking contrasts. Wealth and poverty, beauty and monstrous deformity, side by side. But when you speak of contrasts, you have to maintain some kind of proportion of black and white. If you write about America, I advise you to keep a balance of 'fifty-fifty,' as the Americans say. Don't say that American young people are only interested in baseball and rock-and-roll. They are, of course. They're crazy about them. But believe me, they read newspapers, too, and books and magazines. And they'll read your article when you publish it. Better have that in mind, so later you won't have a red face."

And then there was another journalist, an American this time, one who knows Russian quite well and has visited the Soviet Union several times. He asked me (that was two years later, in Italy) did I plan to write about America. If I did, he said, would I please not end my article with a paragraph about the hard-working, gifted, and courageous people whom the author came to know, in spite of the fact that he was in America only a very short time.

"I'll begin your article at the end," he said. "And if I see that paragraph there, I won't read it. I'll know it can't be objective."

I promised him I would end my article with some other paragraph, and then I asked him how he usually ended his articles on the Soviet Union. He smiled.

"Oh, in different ways," he said. "But once I ended an article just that way: I learned the trick in your country. So I'm warning you."

He wasn't a bad person. He published his articles in a magazine that was not overly sympathetic to the Soviet Union, but I could see that he did keep to the fifty-fifty principle.

Personally, I'm not trying to keep any balance. Besides, I'm doing everything I can to avoid generalizing (I saw too little). I'm only trying to figure out what I did see, the thoughts and associations that came to me as I encountered life in America. I don't pretend to do any more.

Some pages earlier, I was writing about American young people. Did I really get to know them? I only had three meetings with them in the three weeks I was there: first, the Russian Volodya; second, the schoolboys I met on the train; and third, two students from Columbia University. I'm sure I got something out of those meetings. But I wonder how much it really was. Anyway . . .

My meeting with these Columbia students was disappointing. And I'm not sure I understand everything about it. As we left New York for our tour around the country, Tadeusz Osipowicz, our talkative guide, told me that, when we got back to New York, I simply had to go up to Columbia University to meet some of the students in the Russian department there. He said they were very anxious to meet me. Of course, I agreed immediately. What could be more interesting?

On our return to New York—the second day, I think—we all went to Columbia University. Tadeusz Osipowicz urged me again not to forget the students who were looking forward to meeting me. Of course I wouldn't forget. As soon as we arrived, they gave us a very pleasant reception in a little hall for special occasions. There were the customary welcoming speeches, and then we broke up into small groups. The physicists found other physicists, historians found historians, and I set out to look for my own students and the long awaited meeting.

I was accompanied by Professor Mathewson, a teacher of Soviet Russian literature, a middle-aged, hospitable man, who speaks excellent Russian, and has written a book about the positive hero in Soviet literature. He had never heard of the students I was supposed to meet, but he offered to help me find them. We went around to several classrooms, we looked in the library of the Russian department, but there was no one there. We spent a half an hour that way, if not more, stopping to ask people we met, but we didn't find anyone. Why not? I don't know. Professor Mathewson was clearly puzzled (I would even say, embarrassed). Finally, we went into a students' dormitory (like our "Hotel Yunost" * in Moscow, by the way, only a little bigger), but we didn't find them. There were a cheerful lot of youngsters there, running up and down the stairs. They smiled at us pleasantly enough, but when we stopped them, they only shrugged their shoulders and went their way. Disappointed again, we went to the student restaurant.

"Let's sit at that table over there," Professor Mathewson said. "Those look like nice young people."

The young people really were nice, with pleasant, intelligent faces. But I must say, in all my trips abroad, I've never been treated with such indifference. Sipping their coffee, the youngsters gave polite answers to all my questions, but they never asked a single question of their own. I was simply not interesting to them. Just imagine what would happen in one of our university dining rooms if an American came in and sat down at a table, even the most ordinary American, let alone a journalist or a writer. What an argument there would be, how many chairs would be drawn up around him! But nothing like this happened to me. These youngsters were simply bored sitting with me, and none of Professor Mathewson's promptings could change that. I think they both breathed a sigh of relief when we got up to say good-by.

* Literally, *Youth Hotel,* built by members of the Leninist Youth League for students and other young visitors from foreign countries. (*Translator's note*)

And why did this happen? I don't know. I was the first Soviet person these two young American students had ever seen. For a split second when we first sat down, there was a spark of interest in their eyes, but it died out immediately. And yet the schoolboys on the train from Buffalo had been interested in everything: they had asked us a thousand questions.

The film *America Through a Frenchman's Eyes* (people who know America say it captures a great deal) shows many sides of contemporary American youth, American youth at the beaches, doing the rock-and-roll, getting tipsy in amusement parks. Future fathers getting child-care training by practicing on dolls. The good-looking young boys and girls who make their living by having their pictures taken for magazine covers and advertisements. And gloomy young criminals being put behind bars. In Greenwich Village, the Montmartre of New York, I also saw the "high-life" of American youth. One drunken fellow painted all colors of the rainbow, stumbling up and down the sidewalk, shouting that he didn't give a damn who got into the White House, Kennedy or Nixon, it was much more important who was in the Kremlin! All this exists, I know, and there's probably a lot more of it than they show in the film. But somehow I don't like to think it's the only side of American youth. There is another side—I'm sure there is—but I never found it. And that's why I'm so sorry I never met those students, the ones who invited me to Columbia University, the ones I couldn't find. Who was to blame for that? American Express? Ivan Ivanovich? Professor Mathewson? The students themselves? Was I to blame for it? I don't know. But anyway, I don't think it was I. . . .

Of course, it's difficult to judge from just this one experience, but in the two weeks I spent in America, I didn't make friends with a single American. It was quite different in Italy. My "Italian notebook" is full of addresses; my American one has two or three stray telephone numbers. And all this in spite of American sociability and straightforwardness.

I can't help it. When I write about Americans, about their tastes and aspirations, about their likes and dislikes, I shall be writing at second hand. I can only rely on what I have available to me. And so the portrait won't be a very accurate one, and not a very clear one either, as though illuminated by reflected light. But I can't help it.

Art is certainly one of the best reflections.

People who think that Americans are devoted to abstract art, the so-called left-wing art, are very much mistaken. That has never been true. It's true that in the lobby of the New York airport Idlewild there is a many-headed construction that calls itself sculpture, hanging from the ceiling and turning slowly in different directions. (Actually, in itself, I liked it very much. There was a pterodactyl, helicopter quality about it; in other words, the quality of aviation.) There is a special museum in New York, the Solomon R. Guggenheim Museum on Fifth Avenue, devoted mostly to innovational and left-wing art. And there are wealthy collectors in America who will pay anything for the most extreme left-wing fabrications. But the American masses don't like this art: they like art that looks like something.

Now I, for one, am very fond of Polish posters. I think this is the field (like the movies) where the Poles have found their own language, a very expressive language that is all their own. The Polish poster has everything a poster needs: it is striking, memorable, and concise; but first of all, it is a work of art. It has no rhetoric and sermonizing (which unfortunately our poster often has): it is purely visual and poetic. Remember the Polish posters for the Chopin Competition, or the famous anti-war poster *"Nie!"* with only three things in it: a bomb, ruins, and the short, expressive negative. Of course, a poster like this wouldn't work in America. The American poster must be very naturalistic, photographic. The magazines and book covers are the same way. On the walls of skyscrapers, at the entrances to movie houses, and by the side of highways, you see enormous good-looking men and women, gangsters and cowboys, smiling faces and unsmiling ones. And every one of them is carefully done, and what's more important, done with striking realism. There is nothing symbolic about them.

I've been talking about the most utilitarian kind of art because it's the most accessible and it tells you most about public taste. But if you look at higher art forms, for the most part you see a similar tendency. For example, the Marine Corps Monument, which I've already talked about, is very characteristic. Its photographic quality, its realism, is enhanced by the fact that the flag itself is not made out of bronze, but a real American "Stars and Stripes," made of cloth and flapping in the wind.

Yes, this monument arouses definite emotions, very powerful ones, and I've already talked about them. But I wouldn't call it a work of art. It tells the story of a thrilling event. But it has no imagery. And as we know, it's hard to have pictorial art without imagery. (By the way, in Ukrainian, the word *pictorial* means *image-creating*, which I think is very exact.)

Imagery . . . How often we talk about it, and how often we forget that without it there can be no art. Dead water and living water. Dead water can only stick the broken body together, but living water pours life into the soul. The Marine Corps Monument is dead water. But the monument to devastated Rotterdam, that is living water. Many Muscovites will remember its bronze copy, shown at the French Exhibit in 1961. (The original, done by the French sculptor Zadkine, is in Rotterdam.) Most people were revolted by it; they made fun of it, or at the very least, they shrugged their shoulders.

"Is that a man," they said, "or a rusty piece of iron?"

"Why does he have a hole in his stomach?"

"Where is his head?"

"God knows what it is, but it isn't art."

It was painful to listen to them. It was painful to hear them, because the Rotterdam Memorial is a monument to a barbarously decimated city, a monument to thousands of dead bodies. It is a wailing, desolate appeal for justice. It is a frantic, screaming thing. A true work of art, a great work. It is living water.

Living water . . . And we've been getting dead water for so long now.

Not far from each other, on opposite sides of Arbat Square,* there are two statues of Gogol, one by Andreyev and the other by Tomsky. Some time ago, Tomsky's Gogol, pompous and complacent, drove away Andreyev's Gogol, pedestal and all, and took its place. And it stands there to this day. I don't know what other people do, but I always avoid it: I walk across the other side of Arbat Square. And if I have time, I always look into the little courtyard off Nikitsky Boulevard, and there—right next to the house where he died—sitting in meditation, with his coat thrown

* A square in one of the old sections of Moscow, a favorite among Muscovites for its picturesque architecture. (*Translator's note*)

over his shoulders, there is a living Gogol, not a dead one. It's one of the most beautiful statues in the world. I urge the reader to take the few extra steps over to that courtyard and walk around that statue, from Gogol's right shoulder to his left. You will see something extraordinary. Look at his profile, at the side of his face: before you is the Gogol of *Evenings on a Farm Near Dikanka,* gentle, slightly ironic. Walk halfway around him, and you will see him change before your very eyes. From the other side, he's the doubting Gogol, the mystic Gogol, the Gogol of the *Dead Souls* that was burned.* I have never seen such a transformation.

But Andreyev's Gogol was banished. He's found another place to sit now, perhaps a better place. And now let me plead for another statue, another exile, who still hasn't found his rightful place. Taken off his pedestal, he has stood for years already in the yard of the Russian Museum in Leningrad, and no one sees him now: young people don't even know he exists. I'm talking about Alexander III by Paolo Trubetskoy. It's no exaggeration to say this statue is the only one of its kind. I don't know any other that makes such a forceful indictment. In the massive, solemnly self-satisfied figure of the "peace-making" Tsar, sitting in state on a massive dray horse with its feet planted wide apart, you see all the lawlessness of autocratic Russia. At one time, when the statue still stood on Revolution Square in front of the Moscow Station, these lines of Demyan Bedny were carved on its pedestal:

* Gogol began a second part of his novel *Dead Souls* in which he hoped to achieve a truer understanding of good and evil than ever before. Only a few chapters of it survive, however, because shortly before he died, Gogol repudiated his manuscript and burned it. (*Translator's note*)

> *My son and my father were both put to death,*
> *And I live on in their enduring infamy.*
> *Here I protrude, a cast-iron scarecrow,*
> *In a land forever free of the yoke of autocracy.*

That's the statue and it's called the "Scarecrow." But why did they take it away? Whose idea was it? It caused a scandal when it was unveiled in 1909. All the courtiers of the Tsar, Nicholas the Second himself, knew it was a wicked caricature, a satire. Why can't we see that now?

In a separate room in the National Gallery in Washington, there is a painting called "The Last Supper." Its author is Salvador Dali. There are always a lot of people in front of it. And not many paintings are given the honor of a room to themselves.

Salvador Dali is one of the most famous painters of the West. He is a Spaniard, but for the last twenty years he has lived and prospered in the United States. For this reason, even though I don't mean to categorize him as an American painter, I want to say a few words about him.

Salvador Dali is a surrealist. The movement is not a new one, it is at least forty years old. Its best-known representatives are André Breton (he is called the Father of Surrealism), Hans Arp, Max Ernst, Miro, André Masson, Yves Tanguy, and René Magritte. But the most famous of them all, the most sensational, the noisiest, the most extravagant, and, I will even say, the most talented, is Salvador Dali.

He is close to sixty, but he is full of energy. He has a spectacular, spiky mustache, like Wilhelm the Second, which is known all over the world, for Dali loves to have his picture taken. He gives interviews freely; he considers himself something of a philosopher; and he has even written two books: *The Secret Life of Salvador Dali* and *Fifty Secrets of Magic Art*. He loves sensation and all kinds of outrageous pranks.

Somewhere in Italy—I don't remember where, but it's not important—while he was sitting in a loge at a theatrical performance that he himself had created, he blew some kind of gold powder all over the hall. He keeps a piece of paper over his nose while he's working, because he says his nose gets in his way. At one of his exhibits in New York, he had a bathtub placed in a show window, a bathtub lined with wool, with a beautiful woman lying in it. Then he climbed into the showcase, overturned the bathtub, and broke the window. . . .

But all this is just by the way. I've risen to the bait of the American newspapers, and done just as they do, given in to any kind of sensationalism and extravagance of celebrities. Seriously, Dali is an artist, endowed with a refined imagination, an excellent draftsman: all you have to do is look at his pictures to see what a lot of hard work has gone into them. There is no aimless "tail-brushing" here, no "Sunset on the Adriatic" by the notorious donkey.* It's work.

If we are to believe the *Large Soviet Encyclopedia* (*cf.* the article on "Surrealism," volume 41), then "the well-known representative of surrealism, the painter Salvador Dali, paints pictures that glorify atomic war." This is briefly

* A reference to a Futurist exhibit in which a donkey is supposed to have swatted a canvas with a paintbrush tied to his tail. The finished work, "Sunset on the Adriatic," is well known to Soviet people, and reference is often made to it by those who wish to denigrate abstract art, including N. S. Khrushchev at the Moscow Art Exhibit in December, 1962. (*Translator's note*)

and expressively put, but unfortunately, it bears no relation to the truth. Dali, of course, doesn't glorify any sort of war whatever. He doesn't glorify or condemn anything. Salvador Dali, like surrealism itself, is a much more complex phenomenon, even though he is completely consistent with the development of Western art.

I'm not about to deal in detail with the essence of this phenomenon. Undoubtedly, it is in the tradition of Freud and the cult of the unconscious. But I would like to take up another question. When museums and exhibits of abstract art are usually empty, why are there always people crowding around anything by Dali?

As an illustration, let me try to relate one of Dali's paintings (if you can say that about a painting), called "One Second Before Being Awakened by the Buzzing of a Bee Flying Around a Pomegranate." An intriguing title, isn't it? The painting itself is even more so. Above a flat rock like an island, a beautiful woman lies sleeping, suspended in the air. Her arms are raised behind her head, and she is naked. A pomegranate floats in the air beside her. A bee is flying around the pomegranate. Another rock is suspended over her. But this is not the most frightening part. Over the desertlike sea that surrounds the sleeping woman, floats another, larger pomegranate with a bite taken out of it, and all its seeds spilling out. Out of this pomegranate a horrible fish, with huge, gaping jaws, is struggling to break free. Then, out of the fish's maw, leaps an enormous, horrible tiger, with another smaller tiger leaping out of its mouth. Both tigers are just about to sink their teeth into the body of the beautiful woman. And still this is not all. In another second, out of the mouth of the smaller tiger, a rifle with a bayonet will plunge into the woman's outstretched hand. In the background, an elephant stalks the horizon on endlessly long, antennaelike legs, like an insect. On his back he carries an obelisk.

Delirium? Yes, delirium. . . . But that's what the artist is striving for. His world is the world of the nightmare, of hallucination, the world of the unconscious, of the irrational. It's frightening, incomprehensible, but by God, it's entertaining. People crowd around it:

"Look, look at that fish! And the tiger, the tiger looks almost real! And why does the elephant have such long legs? What's that supposed to mean?"

I have to admit that I was interested, too; I also tried to riddle out what the author's "message" could be. It's just a puzzle, a "cross-word." But sometimes you can't tear yourself away from this kind of thing, even though you know you are wasting your time.

The rare craftsmanship of a naturalist, the verisimilitude (the tiger really does look like a living tiger) combined with the irrationality of the subject matter—this is what attracts people by the hundreds. Our tourists, and I among them, spent our last pennies to buy up almost all the postcard reproductions of "The Last Supper" at the National Gallery. This is the painting where, according to the catalogue, Dali "recreates the essence of the twentieth century with lines and forms of classical Catholicism, partly Rennaissance and partly Baroque, with shades of Spanish realism." Now, tell me what that means. (The picture shows the twelve apostles bending over the table, with Christ in the middle, his arms stretched out over all of them, holding the head of Gala, the artist's wife. All this is enclosed in a sort of octahedron which seems to be melting into the air.) Just try to tell me what it means. It's perfectly realistic and incomprehensible at the same time. But anyway . . .

"Let me have a couple more of those post cards."

Both Sides of the Ocean

There has been a great deal written about Salvador Dali. And the people who write about him use such words as "paranoia," "hallucination," "autoerotism," "autosodomy," "psycho-sexuality," "inner-atomic balance," "astral sublimation," and twenty or thirty more as frightening as these. And they write all this in good earnest.

Let me repeat: most of Dali's paintings are striking because of the technical mastery he displays in them, and because of his unrestrained imagination. (Take his series of Madonnas, for example, or the "Santiago El Grande" which was shown in a special pavilion built by Franco's government at the Brussels World's Fair.) But when they try to suggest some supposedly scientific basis for all this, when they try to tell you that Dali "studied the works of Marx and Rosenberg and rejected them, and then went on to recreate the Catholic, European, and Mediterranean traditions which found expression in the colonnades of Bernini, the open embraces (the outstretched arms) of the West, the arms of St. Peter in Rome, in the Vatican," when you read all this, it becomes a little frightening. It's a cul-de-sac.

As I looked at Dali's paintings in the National Gallery and the crowds of people that were always in front of them, I couldn't help thinking of the crowds around some of the paintings at our exhibits, too. In ours, too, everything has been recognizable and unrecognizable at the same time. Dali fled from realism into the dream, to the nightmare, to surrealism. But some of our painters seem to be running just as hard in the other direction, to an antirealism of their own, a carefully flattened, exultingly saccharine kind of antireality.

Fortunately, to some extent, we are already beyond this. But sometimes when you go into certain subway stations

147

or go to the Agricultural Exhibit,* you shudder at the sight of what was once considered the pinnacle of our art. To use the mildest possible expression, we will come to think of it as just as much of a dream.

But the art of America is not painting and not sculpture. The art of America is architecture. Or rather, the genius for construction.

But now let me make a small digression.

Contemporary architecture—both Western and our own —is undoubtedly going through a grave crisis. Ours, on account of a sharp turning point after almost thirty years of the "cult of extravagance." And Western architecture for reasons I'd like to go into at greater length.

I am still puzzled by the creative development of Le Corbusier, Architect Number One, as I heard him called by a passionate young Italian architect, unnumbered himself, with whom I argued in Italy this spring about the current trends in architecture. It seems to me that Le Corbusier's work over the last few years clearly reflects the very crisis that all of Western architecture is going through.

Twenty or thirty years ago, architecture and engineering lived in peace and friendship, helping each other hand in hand. Now a breach has opened between them, and it's becoming wider every day. You would think that architecture (of course, I'm speaking symbolically, in other words, the conceptual side of architecture) has become resentful of engineering.

"You are cramping my style," it says. "I need more room."

And as a result, you get something like the Ronchamp Chapel.

* Held at a large permanent exhibition ground on the outskirts of Moscow with pavilions erected by all fifteen republics displaying the newest agricultural techniques. (*Translator's note*)

I have already written about it. Its fame has resounded all over the world. Its appearance was considered an event of major significance in contemporary architecture. It has even been admitted to the architectural brotherhood of saints. In France it is considered an architectural monument, like Rheims Cathedral or the chateaux of the Loire.

I am trying to understand this chapel. (I am purposely ignoring the basic question: Why did a master, who could say in the years of his blossoming, "What do I have to do with churches? The problems of architecture lie elsewhere, in the building of cities" . . . why did this master take up the architecture of churches in his old age?) Seen from far away, the chapel is white against the picturesque Vosges Mountains. It stands exactly on the spot where its predecessor stood before the war. It is impossible to describe. It is enough to say that it is unlike anything that has ever been built by man. In putting it as crudely as possible, it is a murky cushion lying on curved and sloping white walls. A white stream-lined belfry. And two more smaller ones, standing back to back. (In *First Acquaintance* I made a small sketch of this chapel.)

But let us try to discuss its structure separately from its image. Let's begin with its structure. The walls are made of stone. They are covered over with white plaster, very coarse and rugged, inside and out. The supporting reinforced-concrete structure is also plastered over, like the walls. The building material is of different kinds, all hidden by the general decor, by the plaster. (By the way, the main belfry is not waterproof, so that it is covered with drippings from the rain: at one time Le Corbusier would never have permitted it.) The roof is made of reinforced concrete, not plaster, and the imprint of the frame is left there on purpose. (That's very fashionable now in the West.) Everything, of course, is aimed at contrast. And of the old principles of architecture (you mustn't hide anything; everything must speak for itself) not a trace remains. Apparently, the principles are different now. And at their foundation, there is something new, something that was denied before: the image.

And this is the saddest part of all. Because the image before us must be the image of the irrational. Possibly even of the mystic. The logic of form and of architectural construction has been rejected. And instead we have the allegory of the irrational, the expressive, the inexplicable. Just don't ask questions. Take it as it is. That's all there is to it.

People who have been in the chapel say it is very impressive. The ceiling is dark and sloping, the walls vertical, slanted, and gently curved. The sloping ones open into very deep rectangular slits of different sizes, set about at random (you can't really call them windows), and the sun's rays streaming through them create a striking effect. The panes of glass are clear, but some of them are many-colored, and, according to the architect, they are supposed to give the Chapel the effect of old Romanesque and Gothic architecture. No, apparently it is not that. Apparently, they are meant to arouse similar emotions in the worshipers as were evoked by Gothic architecture and stained-glass windows.

Here is what Le Corbusier himself writes about the Chapel: "Freedom. Ronchamp. The architecture is completely free. No purpose except the celebration of the Mass, one of the most ancient human institutions. The only presence here is the landscape, the four sides of the horizon. It is they that dominate. A true phenomenon of visual acoustics. 'Visual acoustics is a phenomenon that leads into the realm of form.' The forms create sound and stillness: some speak, others listen."

But what does it all mean? True freedom . . . The celebration of the Mass . . . Visual acoustics . . . Sound and stillness . . . What does it mean? Escape from reality again? Irrationality? A new theory?

It seems not. If took five years to complete the Chapel, from 1950 to 1955. During those years and afterward, Le Corbusier designed a government complex in Chandigarh, the capital of Punjab, villas in Ahmedabad, the Brazilian building in the Cité Universitaire in Paris, apartment houses in Neuilly-sur-Seine and Nantes, a museum in Tokyo. And all these designs were based on other principles, principles closer to the old Le Corbusier. Even in the Dominican monastery at Touret, near Lyons, completed in 1959, Le Corbusier paid strict attention to form, perhaps too much attention. And there, too, they "celebrate the Mass . . ."

I'm only sorry about one thing. Le Corbusier was striving for something greater, to build great cities, "a Radiant City," as he called it; but he never lived to see it in reality. And he was dying to work with us.

Here I should like to quote a few passages from the letter Le Corbusier wrote to us architecture students in 1932, the letters I mentioned in my previous book. He refers to the competition for the Palace of Soviets, and the prizes that went to Iofan, Zholtovsky, and the American Hamilton, and bypassed Le Corbusier himself. And here is what he writes:

"The Palace of Soviets should be the crown of the Five-year Plan. It should be the glorification of the architectural principles of the new regime that has inspired that Five-year Plan. . . . The government of the U.S.S.R. commissioned a design from me. The project required all the resources of modern technology. For three months, fifteen designers were busy on the anatomical analysis of the design. Our workshop was all enthusiasm. We devoted ourselves passionately to the finest points and tiniest details. With each new discovery, with each new solution, first one designer and then another would exclaim, 'They'll like this in Moscow!' We all thought the design would be considered from the standpoint of its technical characteristics, from the standpoint of the realities of construction and architecture. The keynotes of our design were: traffic pattern, good visibility, acoustics, ventilation, the statics of the structure.

"And then they made the decision. None of this had been taken into account. The prizes were awarded for sketches of façades, for academic cupolas. . . . Even the judges admitted in the decision that the prize-winning designs gave no instructions on the method to be used for the ceilings, on the acoustics, on the heating, or the ventilation!!!

"The disappointment of our fifteen designers was unimaginable: they were indignant and exasperated."

And from another letter:

"I'm very pleased that the plans for the Palace were commissioned to my friends the Vesninis, but I myself would have liked to work on those parts of it where I feel completely confident. . . . I believe I have some rights to this collaboration, since our design is one of the most serious of all that were submitted."

And finally, the last, the bitterest lines:

"I was invited many times to draw up plans for cities in the U.S.S.R., but it remained just talk. I am very distressed by this, because I feel that I am now in possession of certain truths which I would like to share with others. I have gained such deep insight into basic social truths that I have been the first to create, completely naturally, a great classless city, harmonious and smiling. I am sometimes distressed when I see the U.S.S.R. oppose me on grounds that do not seem sufficient."

We never employed Le Corbusier. We never employed a man who was a very great master, even if he did exaggerate a little in thinking that he had already created a classless city.

It pains me now to see a photograph of Le Corbusier standing on the scaffolding of a monastery under construction, surrounded by monks in soutanes. And who knows, it might never have happened if he could have found a place among different company. Perhaps among the builders of Komsomolsk-on-Amur.

Le Corbusier is the most striking example, but he's not the only one. The abolition of form, the retreat into the irrational—these are not isolated instances, but a regular trend. Very characteristic in this respect is Giovanni Michelucci, the well-known Italian architect who designed many buildings of the thirties, including the Florence railroad station, which was written about a great deal in its time. All these buildings adhered more or less to the regular forms of rationalist-constructivist architecture typical of those years. But now Michelucci has drawn up plans for two churches, the Santa Maria, and the Autostrada-del-Sol. (It is curious that, in our day, the church should be offering architects the greatest freedom.)

I am looking at photographs right now of the sketches and clay models of these two churches, and they leave me without words. I am trying to find something to compare them to, but I can't find anything. The only thing I can say is that they look like something a child might make out of wet sand at the beach. Rambling, sprawling things, sometimes very attractive, like castles or cakes, but mostly incomprehensible. But maybe that's the way to build churches? Well then, let them build them that way. The only trouble is that so many people waste their time on them—and is it only time?—when they could be doing so many more useful things.

I have made this rather long digression to lead up to what I want to say about the architecture of America.

I have often been asked if I like it, and I have answered that I do. And that's what I answer now:

"Yes, I do like it."

I see a look of surprise.

"What do you mean? Americans themselves don't know how to get out of the mess they've made. Talk about a cul-de-sac, there's a perfect example: an insoluble transportation problem, no light, no air, an elevated railway in Chicago that would drive the strongest man out of his mind. The skyscrapers only look good on post cards and the only ones who admire them are the tourists. . . ."

All that is true, but still . . .

A friend and I wandered along the shore of Lake Michigan in Chicago. It snowed the night before, snow mixed with rain. The city was covered with mist, reddish yellow in the light from the advertising signs, its wet asphalt glistening. But now the weather cleared. The sun was shining and the lake—wide as a sea—was quietly curling its waves over the cold, deserted beach. All around, it was surprisingly, improbably empty. There were cars sweeping by—low, wide, noiseless—but no people. We were alone on that endless beach. There was no reason for a Chicagoan to be there; the summer was over, and the beach was closed. (And what a beach! We could do with one like it in Yalta.) And that barren landscape, that idyllic stillness, gave us a chance to see the city, the most American of all cities, more American than New York, to stand back a moment and have a good look at it, without haste, without hurrying to get anywhere, sitting on the parapet, smoking cigarettes, letting our conversation lazily bandy back and forth.

On one side of the lake (the fourth largest in the world, not counting the Aral Sea) the wind came up and the surface was full of ruffles. On the other side, the row of skyscrapers of the "Gold Coast," the most fashionable section of Chicago. Among them, two dark, vertical shapes. I recognized them from pictures I had seen. They are famous. They were built by one of America's most illustrious architects, Mies Van der Rohe. Beautiful! My God, they were beautiful. There's a city for you!

Now we walk across a bridge, over dozens of railroad tracks, strings of trains moving, freights and passengers, semaphores blinking, cars speeding noiselessly over the bridge, two workers in cradles, screwing light bulbs into one of the "o's" of a giant "Coca-Cola." (Why did we make fun of it? It's really a delicious and refreshing drink.) Before us now is another panorama, the skyscrapers of Michigan Avenue, stretching on for over a mile. At their head, the newly built Prudential Building. Right now it is all ablaze: the low November sun is gleaming in the windows of every one of its forty-odd stories. We continue along the shore, and then turning down Madison Street, we find ourselves in the very center of town, at the loop. (The overhead railway, the "elevated," actually does make a loop at this point.)

The advertising signs are on twenty-four hours a day, and yet it is always semidarkness here. The shopwindows are all aglow with their shimmering wares. On the corner, by the staircase leading up to the elevated, there is a stack of newspapers with the results of the presidential election. People grab them as they run by, and throw five cents into a little tin box. The gray skyscrapers loom overhead. Some forty years ago, Harold Lloyd was jumping from one to the other. . . .

A city . . . A gigantic city. The largest railway center, 1,700 trains a day! America's second city. The famous slaughterhouses, canning houses, iron, and steel. The birthplace of the American Communist party. The city that gave us the First of May, after the demonstration of 1886 was fired on. A city which had 4,000 people 125 years ago and now has 5½ million. A city which went up in flames in 1871 and now is careful to keep outside fire escapes on all the skyscrapers. A city of financiers, magnates, clerks, and workers. A real city. A gigantic city.

But the architecture? How does the architecture fit into all this? And how can you say you like it? The gloomy streets, the fire escapes?

First of all, I'm a city person, and I like the dramatic urbanism of these cities. I like the skyscrapers, all glass and steel, reflecting the clouds drifting across the sky. I like to look up and see their vertical edges, precise as a mathematical formula. I like their disorder, their commotion, breaking up the regularity of the streets. I'm talking about the appearance of the city. Not its tragedy. I'm not talking about whether it's dirty, hot, suffocating, whether the gasoline fumes are stifling. I don't care if its layout is haphazard or well-thought-out, whether its style is pure or not. I'm talking about how it looks.

I understand that it is necessary to keep a regularity when we build Southwest Moscow. But the Moscow I love is not the Moscow of Lomonosov Avenue, or Vernadsky Avenue. It is the tangle of bystreets around Arbat Square, and, grown among them for good or for ill, the tall building on Smolensk Street. For me, Moscow is Krechetnikovsky Lane, living out its last days. It is Sobachya Square. It is the House of the Moscow Processing Trust with the lines from Mayakovsky that some overzealous building manager plastered on it. It is Tversky Boulevard with its pensioners playing chess, and the children playing in the sand. "Hotel Moscow" (even though I still remember Okhotny Ryad * with its old church and its stalls for produce). The subway station, "Revolution Square" with its statues of boys and girls, so naïve and still so dear to our hearts, bringing back so many memories. My Moscow is Andreyev's statue of Gogol. St. Basil's. Red Square.

Here I imagine what an old-time New Yorker might say, sighing nostalgically:

"New York, I remember you when all this bustle and hurry didn't exist, when stately carriages rolled leisurely along Fifth Avenue instead of hurrying, when pigeons cooed on Times Square, and the Singer Company Building was the tallest in the world. Now you can't even find it among all the glass boxes around it. And for three cents, the trolley took you all over Manhattan. And you didn't have to suffocate in those dark, stuffy dungeons."

But it's not a question of what a city used to be like and

* Literally, Hunter's Row, an open-air market formerly on the site of the Hotel Moscow. (*Translator's note*)

how it's changed. I'm talking about how a city looks, its uniqueness and its charm. The Leningrad canals, the white nights, the spire on the Admiralty building, the gloomy Dobuzhinsky*-Dostoevskian yards with their sheds for firewood. All these are as unique as the Polenovian ** courtyards in Moscow against a background of construction cranes and prefabricated houses: contemporary Moscow. As unique as the steep Dnieper Hills in Kiev, or Andreyevsky Drive, slowly crawling up the hill on its own cobblestones. As unique as the backyards of Odessa with their balconies and laundry hung out to dry. This uniqueness is where you find a city's character, its charm, and its soul.

I have seen many impersonal cities in America, one just like the other: Detroit, Buffalo, and others: they're all blended together in my memory. But not New York and not Chicago. They are foreign to me, perhaps, but they have their own charm, their own soul.

Once, very early in the morning, I walked along the streets in the dock district along the Hudson. The endless fences of the warehouses stretched out with their enormous billboards, there were switch engines whistling just the way ours do, and ragged cats lingering in the streets. And then suddenly, as I turned up a side street, I saw the Empire State Building. . . . It was wrapped in the early morning mist, but the upper stories were already reddening in the sunlight and the windows were gleaming. All around, other enormous shapes, only slightly smaller, were waiting for the sun to strike them, too. And down below, in the can-

---

* M. S. Dobuzhinsky (1875–1957), Russian painter, stage designer, and illustrator of Dostoevsky, famous for his views of the Russian metropolis. (*Translator's note*)
** V. D. Polenov (1844–1927), Russian landscape and portrait painter. (*Translator's note*)

yons between them, the chilly morning vapors melted away. . . . That morning I understood the beauty of that huge, contradictory city, the beauty of its glass and steel, the beauty of its architecture. . . .

We usually think that the architecture of America is the architecture of skyscrapers. In a way it's true, and in a way it isn't. Of course, it's true that the Americans invented the skyscraper. They perfected the design, the functional-esthetic forms, of which the Seagram Building in New York by Mies Van der Rohe, or the Lever House (Skidmore, Owings, and Merrill) are the crowning examples. But the skyscraper is only one feature of America's architecture, or rather, as I said before, the American genius for construction.

By this term I mean not only the scope of their building technique, but their ability to combine the architecture of the buildings with the architecture of "engineering." Bridges of striking beauty and lightness, (the Golden Gate in San Francisco or the George Washington in New York), viaducts that intersect each other at different levels, and highways, I would even say, have all become an integral part of the contemporary American landscape.* All these

---

* Frank Lloyd Wright wrote: "I foresee that roads too will become architecture, because they are fully capable of becoming that—great architecture."

things together are what make up the architecture of America—confused and at the same time purposeful, over-whelming and bewitching, mathematically exact and an-archic. This is the essence of it. And its fascination. And the trouble with it . . .

But architecture is not only buildings; architecture is the people who create it. In America, these people are Frank Lloyd Wright, Richard Neutra, Mies Van der Rohe, Eero Saarinen, Aalto, Oscar Niemeyer and finally, Walter Grop-pius, who has lived and worked in the United States since 1937. The architectural thought of the present century owes a great deal to these world-famous masters. I won't weary the reader by a list of everything they have done. (The most brilliant event of recent years was the construc-tion of the capitol of Brazil, the city of Brasilia designed by Niemeyer and Lucio Costa.) But I do want to say a few words about one of the greatest architects of the end of the nineteenth and beginning of the twentieth centuries, Frank Lloyd Wright, who died in 1959 at the age of ninety.

Wright was an American, but he did not build skyscrap-ers. "The greatest architect in the world," as Americans call him, achieved his fame precisely as an opponent of the skyscraper. Instead, he developed his own theory, the theory of "organic architecture." *

"What I ask for in architecture," he wrote in one of his articles, "is exactly what I ask for in a human being: sin-cerity and inner truthfulness. In these are all the qualities in architecture for me."

---

* Three years before he died he couldn't resist any longer and he designed a skyscraper for Chicago: the *Illinois,* 528 stories and over 5,000 feet high. All the plans and sketches for it are done, but it remains a question whether it will ever be built.

In practice, this meant that an architectural structure should not contrast with the surrounding countryside, but on the contrary, it should enhance it, should become an organic part of it. As a result, most of Wright's buildings, especially the villas, are all built on flat country (there is even a term for them, "The Prairie-Style"), designed in horizontals, subordinated to the contours of the place and at the same time emphasizing them. He also used local materials in construction: rough-hewn stone contrasting sharply with the plate-glass windows and the reinforced-concrete roofs that stretch out in horizontals.

Frank Lloyd Wright built a great deal in his lifetime, more than eleven hundred buildings, not counting several hundred more that have not been executed. There were many contradictions in his creative art—he had his ups and downs—but on the whole, his influence on world architecture both in theory and practice has been enormous.

Wright's last creation, his swan song, was the Solomon R. Guggenheim Museum on Fifth Avenue in New York. It was opened in 1960.

Often we like to compare unusual objects with familiar ones. They said the Schusev Theater in Rostov looked like a tractor, that something else looked like an airplane. Well, the Guggenheim Museum doesn't look like anything at all. (Some of our tourists did say that it reminded them of a steamship, others of a washing machine.) It is an enormous white spiral made of reinforced concrete, growing wider toward the top, and resting on a broad horizontal base. The rest of the dimensions complement and emphasize the basic ones.

The enormous spiral is the museum itself. You go up in an elevator to the very top, and then, around the spiral itself, which is actually a gallery with a courtyard in the middle—you walk down again. It is 4,000 feet long. I have never seen a museum arranged more rationally, or more conveniently, both for the viewers and the displays. The paintings hang in a single row, at eye level, but to be exact, they don't really hang there: they are fastened to the wall by brackets, which creates the illusion that they are suspended in the air against the background of the white wall. There is a lot of air, and a lot of light (both natural and artificial, and the two are blended together very subtly), a lot of greenery, and even a pool with a little fountain.

The museum has a rich and varied collection. Cezanne, Modigliani, Leger, Picasso, Paul Klee, Kandinsky, Chagall, sculptures by Lipchitz and Brancusi: in short, all the most interesting artists the West has produced since the end of the nineteenth century. And I must say the art work and the architecture are fused together perfectly. The pictures and sculptures fit in comfortably and have plenty of room. They are right at home.

Frank Lloyd Wright sang his swan song and died. But the strange part is that the song was unlike all the music he had created during his life. He had never been a constructivist, and yet his swan song was a hymn to constructivism. In the second half of the twentieth century, he reared a building on the corner of Eighty-ninth Street and Fifth Avenue that Le Corbusier would have been glad to sign his name to, that is, if he had not repudiated what he himself had engendered. It is a beautiful, intelligent building, and it will have a place in every textbook of architecture, but it is not Wright.

An entire issue of the Italian magazine *L'Architettura* (Volume 82, August, 1962) is completely devoted to the twenty-fifth anniversary—no, not of the architect, but one of his works, "The House by the Waterfall," *"Falling Water."*

"The House by the Waterfall" is the villa of the Detroit millionaire Edgar Kaufmann, who thought he'd like a house built on that very spot, at Bear Run, Pennsylvania, in that forest, beneath that very waterfall. And he wanted Frank Lloyd Wright to build it for him. And so Wright built it.

"The plan of a house is a way of life," said Wright. "And a way of life is always an individual matter." And so he built this beautiful villa to conform with Kaufmann's way of life.

There is a thin, scanty woods on the hillside, a brook, rocks, and a waterfall. And over this waterfall, hanging over it by its terraces, is the house itself. Although it adheres to Wright's theory of "organic architecture," "the most significant part of its design (the reason why the house was built), is its internal space, not the covering of that space, that is, the walls and roofs, and especially not its external appearance." This villa, whose external appearance has, indeed, received so much attention, completely fulfills another of Wright's theses: "Internal space is a part of the single space of nature, and therefore it should not close itself off from the space around it, but become unified with it as much as possible." Wright was able to achieve this unity completely. The villa grew into the landscape, or maybe it grew out of it: it became an organic part of it. The rocks of the brook and the rough stone walls of the house, the white horizontal terraces and the intersecting verticals of the trees, the repose of comfort and the thunder and spray of the waterfall, all these are merged into the unity and pervade the interior of the house. Inside, the same natural stone (no plaster here!) and the wall-sized panes of glass seem to draw the surrounding landscape into the house itself. All this was planned to the most minute detail, down to the place near the fireplace for an armful of wood.

Like Le Corbusier at one time, Wright believed that social life could be reorganized with the help of architecture (and also, perhaps, of religion). He was a rebel all his life. He criticized American democracy, the American way of life, the capitalist ethic. He felt he ought to serve the people, and he always wanted to build low-cost housing for ordinary American families. But things worked out differently for him. He became a "fashionable" architect, and he built luxurious villas for millionaires. . . .

Wright criticized the capitalist system. ("Our prosperity is a fraud," he said.) And at the First Congress of Soviet Architects, he said that he was taking away with him "an impression of the greatest achievements and the greatest hope—the greatest I have ever had—for mankind and the future of the earth." But as soon as he got back from Moscow, he hurried off to Bear Run to build his little *chef-d'oeuvre*.

I am deeply convinced that this time, too, we missed an opportunity to employ the knowledge and mastery of one of the world's greatest architects. Furthermore, if we had invited him to work with us, we would have helped him to realize his cherished dream of building for the people. Kaufmann may be a splendid person, but all the same, it seems a pity to waste the talent of a master like Wright, so that thanks to him, Mr. Kaufmann can spread out on his chaise longue and shout over the noise of the waterfall:

Old man Wright didn't slap together a bad little shack, did he?

That passionate young Italian architect I mentioned, the unnumbered one, told me during our argument over architecture:

"Last year I was in Moscow. There was a lot I liked there, but one thing I couldn't understand. What do you want skyscrapers for? In America there is a need for them. Even in our country it's understandable. Land is expensive. But you? What do you need them for? For their looks? Pretty expensive looks, don't you think?"

I said they certainly were expensive, and God knows, architecturally those tall buildings don't have much value, but in their own way they are a special monument of the times. As we all know, they are the "chronicle of history in stone." And I went on in the same vein.

The chronicle of history in stone. . . . Now it's not in stone, it's a chronicle in reinforced concrete, in steel, a pre-constructed, framed and paneled chronicle, a chronicle of a system, of a social order.

In one of those letters I mentioned, Le Corbusier wrote:

"From a distance the USSR seems to be the scene of great activity in the field of architecture. The whole world believes that your country is where the new architecture is being born."

Le Corbusier was not exaggerating. Thirty years ago that was really true. We were far poorer than we are now, and we were a little short on experience, but as far as creative thought was concerned, we were bubbling over with it. Then came the turning point, the competition for the Palace of Soviets, and for two and a half decades since then, everything has been going backward. (I well remember the years of that sudden change: I got a "troika" * on my thesis because I refused to repudiate constructivism.) But thank God, those years are behind us now. Now everything suggests we are entering a new era, an era of new building materials, new designs, new techniques: a new contemporary architecture.

A new contemporary architecture? What does that mean?

About two years ago the *Literary Gazette* commissioned me to do an article on "architectural questions." I wrote the article and tried to unravel some questions of theory, but for some reason the article was a long time coming out. Apparently, the editorial board called together an "architectural colloquium" and together they all discussed my work. Some of them praised it and others criticized it. Finally, the article was published, but before the issue came out, one of the editors said to me:

"Here's the thing, you see. Won't we be letting the young people down? They say, 'Everything has changed now. Now we can build in a new way. Why do we need to theorize? Constructivism, neo-constructivism, formalism, neo-formalism. If we go into all those "isms" again, we'll get all tangled up. All we want to do is build.' "

* The Soviet grading scale is numbered five through one, so that Nekrasov's "three" is equivalent to a C. (*Translator's note*)

I'm not sure that young people in architecture really think this way. Perhaps a small minority of them do. But one thing is clear, our theory is not in very good shape right now: that is more or less obvious.

But maybe we really can let it wait a while? We will find our way ultimately; but for the time being the important thing is to build, build, build. . . . And we are building. We are building a great deal. There are some sections in Moscow now which you simply don't recognize. You go there looking for a house you visited just a little while ago, but this time you get lost, you can't find the way any more.

But still one could wish we were building not only rapidly and in great volume, but practically and comfortably as well, and most important, attractively.

Our construction is very different from construction in the West. We have an unlimited capacity for standardization, for the mass production of building materials. This is the source of our strength, but it is the source of our problems, too.

"A city should be built in such a way that every part of it, every mass of buildings taken by itself, should create a living landscape. Every group of buildings must have a play to it, so that, if you can put it that way, it should play on its own distinctions, should etch itself suddenly into your memory and haunt your imagination afterwards. There are some sights you can remember for a lifetime, and some you hardly even notice."

This is what Gogol wrote a hundred and thirty years ago in his essay, "On the Architecture of Our Time." Gogol had his own views on architecture. He believed that a city should be made up of houses built in all styles existing in the realm. He even imagined a street which would be "an architectural chronicle in itself," a street "which to some extent would make up the history of style, where anyone who is too lazy to turn the pages of heavy volumes could simply stroll up and down to learn everything." I'm not sure how good a city planner Gogol would have made, but when he says, for example, that "the new cities have no character: they are so regular, so facile, and so monotonous that you feel bored walking down one street and lose all interest in seeing another," you can't help asking yourself, "How could Gogol have been in the Novye Cheremushki in Moscow or our Chokolovka in Kiev?" *

In the architecture of a city, the picturesque is a difficult question. Prague is one of the most picturesque cities in the world, where the Gothic, the baroque, and the ultracontemporary live together in peaceful harmony on the same green hills. But it took centuries to build. The carelessness, the haphazard nature of its skyline is magnificent. The view of the roofs and belfries of the Stare Mesto and the Mala Strana, seen from Hradcany Hill, is irresistible. But a skyline can't be made to look haphazard. In this respect, hillside cities have an advantage: the contours of the land itself are a help to the architect. But what about cities built on level ground?

The Romans are very proud of their new suburbs, where new apartment buildings are going up by the dozens. Well, they may be very nice to live in. (I was in two or three of the apartments and they looked very comfortable and convenient.) But all the same, how plain everything looks around them. What tiresome uniformity . . .

I think there is one solution for this. Standardized architecture can be enhanced by many other things, by color,

* Newly built residential sections in Moscow and Kiev with impersonal, uniform buildings. (*Translator's note*)

painting, sculpture, greenery, incidental objects. We have already made some progress in this direction, not great progress perhaps, but noticeable enough. Monumental-decorative art is gradually beginning to work together with architecture. One of the most successful examples, in my opinion, is the new bus terminal in Kiev. (The architects were A. Miletsky, I. Melnik, E. Bilsky; the artists were V. Melnichenko and A. Rybachuk.) Here is something that has found its own way, something fresh, unhackneyed. This is no painting from the Agricultural Exhibit, no mosaic paneling from the Moscow subway. It is something that goes hand in hand with architecture.

On all three stories of the station, the walls and columns are in mosaic. There is a wall of glazed ceramic tile, black, with colored stripes running through it horizontally—movement!—the outline of automobiles racing in different directions. Here and there, little graffitto panels: a road, a highway, a city street with lampposts, cars rushing toward you. The columns are faced with mosaics of green majolica: a bus suddenly flashes by, a chestnut tree in bloom rises suddenly among the geometrical lines. . . .

If you ever have a chance to be in this bus station, go into the restaurant (by the way, the food's not bad there) and have a look at the walls. Then go into the children's nursery—if they let you in. What cute, amusing drawings you will see. And don't miss the curtains on the windows: they, too, were specially made to order. And then go into the accommodations for the passengers: I'll bet you put off your departure for at least twenty-four hours.

Maybe I go on too long about this bus terminal: It was built by friends of mine. But my God, when people build not only with knowledge but with devotion, too (Ada Rybachuk and Volodya Melnichenko spent nights gluing the mosaics on the columns, and Miletsky the architect still comes over to the terminal to be sure that the armchairs in the waiting room are in the right place and that no one has pinched any of the made-to-order ceramics from the passenger's rooms), under these conditions, it's hard to build badly. There is no lack of enthusiasts among our architects. If our building material were only a bit better, of better quality, we would have something to brag about.

Still, our theory is in bad shape. But there is such a thing as the Academy of Construction and Architecture, and there are specialists there working on it. Let us wish them success.

It was evening. Niagara Falls was cascading and thundering beneath us. On the Canadian side, searchlights were turning it alternately pink, green, blue, violet, and white. It was a beautiful sight, but at the same time a pathetic one. They had harnessed the waterfall to serve the tourists; and humbly, patiently, it was doing its work. Nearby shone the lights of an impersonal, boring little town, Niagara Falls: a tourist town.

We were getting ready to go back to the hotel (We had to go on to Buffalo, to visit a dentist's office. That was on the schedule.) when a tall man came toward us, wearing a jacket with the collar turned up.

"I hear the Russian language," he said. "You are Russians, yes?"

"We are."

"Oh, then I may have a talk with you, yes? I am Ukrainian. My name is Dimitry Korinetz. I have a long time not heard the Russian language."

He took out a pack of cigarettes. "Allow me."

I took out my pack of Dnieper-Cossacks.

He smiled.

"Take it," I said.

He tried to pull out a cigarette between two fingers.

"No, the whole thing."

"What? The whole thing?"

"Yes, take it."

"The whole pack?"

"The whole pack."

My God, he was happy! He put the cigarette back, and then he wrapped up the pack in his handkerchief and put it in his pocket. No, he wasn't going to smoke them now. He would only smoke them on special occasions. He would keep them for a souvenir. From Kiev. Just think, cigarettes from Kiev, *Dnieper-Cossacks*. He himself was a Dnieper-Cossack. All Ukrainians are. Well, not all of them. But most of them are.

He took us back to the hotel. He insisted that we should go to the bar. We would all sit down together. We would have a chat. In just a second he would run home and change his clothes. He had just come from work and he hadn't had time to change.

But we couldn't go to the bar. . . . Why not? . . . Because we had to go to the dentist's.

How sorry he was. And I was sorry. We would have all sat down together, we would have had a talk. . . .

I don't remember what work he did. In some kind of business. Anyway, he wasn't happy with it. On the other side, in Canada, things were better. Had we been in Canada? No, we came by train from Chicago. If we wished, he would get a taxi, and in three minutes we would be in Canada. "There's a better view of the falls from there, and the bars are cheaper. . . . Oh, let the dentist wait a while. He's not going to die before you get there."

But we were not allowed to go to Canada. Tadeusz

Osipowicz had very strictly forbidden it. Thirty paces from the hotel, Korinetz made his last try to take us to the bar: "Just five minutes, no more. They have vodka there, and . . ."

But Ivan Ivanovich gave me an anxious and peremptory look, and I was forced to refuse once again.

We could have all sat down together, we could have had a talk. . . .

We said good-by to Korinetz at the entrance to the hotel. How he hated to go. Just think, his first meeting in forty years with a man from Kiev, from his beloved Kiev. He had never been there himself. He was born in America. But he loves Kiev. He pays his deepest respects to it. To Kiev he makes a low bow.

We parted.

A Russian abroad. A Ukrainian abroad. For most of these people, this is a tragedy.

In New York I met a woman I had known before. The last time I saw her was before the war, in 1938 or 1939. She had lived through the occupation with her ten-year-old son. Her husband was at the front. As the Germans retreated, they drove the local population ahead of them. She and her son were herded into a troop train. Along the way, it was badly bombed, and they lost each other. The son made his way home somehow. The mother disappeared.

And now here I had met her in New York, after more than twenty years. Neither of us had grown any younger, but we recognized each other. We sat in Central Park together, and she told me what had happened to her. Why hadn't she gone home? That is always a hard question. She was afraid. At that time, after the war, people were saying all kinds of things. She had been liberated by the Americans, and so she came to America. She knew nothing of her family. She had written letters. Nobody answered them. Probably they had a different address now.

She has a job. She earns good money. She has friends here, too. But she longs to be home. She has a son there, and a granddaughter. Maybe she wouldn't be a burden to them. She could look after her granddaughter.

I visited her at her house. There was a photograph of her son on the wall: it showed him as a little boy; and he must be thirty years old now. There were pictures of Kiev, Vladimir Hill, the Dnieper, all cut out of Ukrainian-American magazines. She treated me to borscht, real Ukrainian borscht.

We said good-by in a little coffee shoppe in midtown New York. I was in a hurry to get back to the hotel. The others were waiting for me: in one hour the bus would leave for the airport. She was writing a letter to her son. She couldn't finish it up. Always thought of something else she wanted to say.

"One second, one second. I'll be through right away."

Then we said good-by. I put the envelope in my pocket, and hurried into the street. I turned and waved back at her. Through the glass door, you could see the inside of the coffee shoppe. She was sitting at the same table, crying. All my life I will remember that clear autumn evening, the small New York coffee shoppe with the swinging glass door, and the woman at the table, crying. I wonder if I'll ever see her again. I wonder if she'll ever see her son.

It's a tragic story, and yet how many like it are there in the world? Life is especially hard for anyone who can't forget his native land.

About three months ago I received a letter from Perth, Western Australia, with a neatly printed invitation to the wedding of a young man who had been a year and a half old when I last saw him. Then came another letter with a picture of the smiling young couple. Next to the fiancé was his mother, the daughter of a well-known Kiev artist: she and I had been classmates in a dramatic workshop many years before.

The war separated the daughter from her parents, drove her to the opposite end of the earth. Now the parents are in Kiev, the daughter in Australia. For fifteen years they knew nothing of each other. Then suddenly, a letter. A letter from the southern hemisphere to the old address in Kiev: by a miracle it was still the same one.

"Don't ask me why I never wrote," she says. "I couldn't explain it. Even now I'm writing in the dark. I don't even know if you are alive."

What happened to make her finally write this letter. After fifteen years . . . A fantastic story. She was just beginning to forget her native city, when one day she happened to drop into a bookstore in Perth. (Until last year, I had never even heard of this place.) She saw a book on the shelf. . . . No, it's almost impossible to believe: on the shelf there was a book, the memoirs of her father, published in Kiev in the Mistiestvo Publishing House in 1959. . . . She could hardly believe her eyes. On the first page there was a portrait of her father. He had grown old now, and gray. But it was her father. Her father. . . . And so she wrote the letter.

She had no peace from that day on. All her thoughts were of Kiev.

"Send me anything, as long as it's about Kiev. Post cards,

albums, photographs. Write me. Tell me what the streets look like now. Tell me what has changed in all these years. Write me everything. Write me."

She has one dream now—to be home again. But how? She has no money and not much of her old energy. And the most frightening part is that it's been so long, she might find herself a stranger in her native land. And what about her son? He grew up in Australia, got used to it, became an Australian, and now he's just married an Australian girl. How hard it is! How infinitely hard!

"But write me. Write me as often as possible. Every letter from Kiev is a joy. The greatest joy in the world."

In the photograph, I see a twenty-five-year-old boy in a dark suit and a bow tie, with a dignified smile. He looks respectable enough, but from what his mother says, it's only the way he looks. In twenty-five years, he's managed to change jobs about ten times: he's worked in a gold mine, a bakery, and repairing radios; he's tinkered with engines, taken refrigerators apart and put them together, and been a foreman in a store. His latest craze is a motorcycle. And naturally, first chance he got, he sailed into a telephone pole and smashed his face in. But he's all right now; his face healed over.

"He's a good boy," his mother says. "The only thing is that he didn't want to finish school. He's very interested in Russia and he likes the Soviet system, but he's afraid if he goes there, they'll make him go to school, and that doesn't appeal to him a bit. He prefers to have a job. Here in Australia, the young people wait until they're fourteen years old and then they quit school and get a job, any job: in a store or an office, or a garage, or a factory. The girls get jobs in hospitals. They're all dying to get working, to save money, to get a car, and get married. What do you need a profession for, when you can get a job without it? My son's just like everyone else. But he's really a good boy. And a good comrade. The ship *Vitiaz* came to our port, and on the second day he was on a second-singular basis with all the young people in the crew. But you'll see for yourself. He'll write you."

And really, he did write me, a letter of almost twenty lines.

"I don't know whether to use the second person plural or the second person singular," he begins, "but in my opinion it doesn't matter very much. So I'll use the singular." Then, a moment later, he finishes up: "Next time I'll try to write a little more. My best regards to your mother, to everyone, to you (the you is crossed out)."

Now he looks at me from the photograph with his slender smile. Next to him is a young woman in a wedding dress with a bouquet of roses. The picture was taken in Perth, Western Australia. That sort of thing happens, I suppose.

As we came out of the airplane in Brussels, after a six-hour flight from New York, we were met by a friendly, smiling, heavy-set man, who immediately introduced himself: "Mamonov, Alexander Vasilievich."

He was a Sabena Airline guide, who offered his services for the two days we had to spend in Belgium before we could take the plane to Moscow.

It's hard to find words to describe the care and attention that this son of a Russian admiral devoted to us. He was most concerned that we should not be bored in Brussels and that we should see as much of it as we could in the two days we had there. Besides the sights of Brussels, he showed us the Congo Museum (about twenty kilometers outside the city). And he even managed to drive us to

Antwerp, the city of sea gulls dying in the harbor. On the way back from Antwerp, even though it was already very late, he stopped the bus at a crossroads, and with a sly wink, he said, "Well, what about going to Waterloo."

And so we went to Waterloo.

The famous battlefield was already closed, but Alexander Vasilievich stole off somewhere, slipped something into the right palm, and in a moment all doors were open before us. Actually, there was nothing very special to see: a lot of busts of Napoleon. And to make it worse, we didn't even get to see the battlefield because a pelting rain came down suddenly. But Alexander Vasilievich was beaming from head to foot. He had squeezed as much as possible out of the day for us, everything that could have been squeezed out of it.

The next morning, just before our take-off for Moscow, he solemnly appeared with his wife and gave us each a souvenir, a scarf with a view of Brussels printed on it, or a tiny gilded statue of "Manneke-Pis" the famous Brussels sculpture, erected to commemorate a remarkable event in the life of one of the crown princes: the poor fellow had long suffered from a kidney stone, then, at last, he was relieved of it. For years, the charming little child has been attracting crowds of inquisitive tourists.

Alexander Vasilievich is not a professional guide. He owns an antique shop, and makes his living from it. He works as a guide only because he loves Russians.

"Only this way do I have a chance to see you," he said, "and travel with you, and talk with you, and ask you questions."

When he learned that I had once been an architect, he promised to send me some books that would interest me. I had hardly reached home, when a large package arrived from Brussels: a beautiful edition of the work of Le Corbusier. And then in two more weeks, another one came, even more beautiful. Wasn't it touching? Thank you, Alexander Vasilievich. Maybe someday you will visit your old country. And I promise you we will try to return all your kind attention, all your care.

Speaking of Mamonov, I can't forget our revered Tadeusz Osipowicz, who was with us constantly for two entire weeks. We got along with him pleasantly enough, even though he treated me a little mistrustfully, without losing his sense of humor, of course. For some reason or other, he thought I had mischievous eyes, and he decided that I was never to be relied on in any serious matter. All the same, we got along together.

He would show up every morning wearing his customary bow tie, clean-shaven, alert, smiling. And walking around our breakfast table he would announce cheerfully: "Today, my friends, we have a slight change. Instead of the Modern Art Museum, we will go first to the Metropolitan, and then . . ."

A murmur went round the table. Everyone had made his own plans and now had to change them in a hurry. There was some haggling about the means of transportation—who was going on foot, who by bus, who by subway—but finally it all got settled, and with a clap of the hands from Tadeusz Osipowicz—"Come on, let's go, we don't have much time" —we headed off, wherever we had to go.

On the way, he expounded his commentary. It usually came in three variations. First, "the old houses are being torn down and new ones are taking their place." Second, "the Negro population of the city has reached such and such a figure, and very soon it will move out of the slums and into better living quarters." And third, any statue we saw of anybody not riding a horse was automatically a statue of Columbus. On this third point, he had convinced us so completely that whenever we saw a statue, we would say, "Let's just walk as far as that Columbus over there and rest a little."

Like Ivan Ivanovich, he didn't like deviations from the schedule and unnecessary questions. Once when we were driving up Fifth Avenue, I saw the outline of a familiar building.

"Tadeusz Osipowicz, what is that?"

He dismissed it with a wave of his hand. "Oh, that's a museum of someone called Solomon. It's not very interesting . . ."

And so we discovered the Guggenheim Museum. And Tadeusz Osipowicz was absolutely reluctant to take us into it.

"Oh, we'll only get lost again, and we'll be late for dinner, and really, there are just a bunch of sloppy paintings in there."

In defense of Tadeusz Osipowicz, we must admit that on the art question he takes the position of the most orthodox critic in our Academy of Artists.

Our parting was a sad one. For some reason, Tadeusz Osipowicz suddenly took offense. I was sitting with a couple of friends at Idlewild Airport waiting for the plane to Europe, when he came up to us, without his customary sense of humor, and delivered us a short tirade.

"Frankly, I'm not only hurt, I'm simply amazed," he said. "You are not the first Soviet tourist group I've ever had. And always, on the day they leave, they give me a present of a bottle of 'Capital.' It's not the vodka I care about, because you know I don't drink. But I like to go back to the office and show off the bottle and say, 'Look how my Soviet tourists expressed their gratitude.' You are the first group I have ever had that didn't give me any vodka. I am bitterly offended."

Then he turned sharply, and walked away. Later, at the gate to the airfield, he shook everyone's hand, and without looking us in the eyes, he pronounced with supreme reserve: "Bon voyage."

Dear Tadeusz Osipowicz! God knows if we will ever meet again. I don't know your address, so let me say a few words to you here. I'm very sorry that you were offended. But on my word of honor, you were to blame for it yourself. If you hadn't marched up to us with your acrid speech, we would have bid you very heartfelt farewell. We had even rehearsed it a little. I had a book all ready for you, with an inscription I thought was very witty. And then you marched up and spoiled everything. Why? Why? Ay-ay-ay. And besides—let's keep this between ourselves—one of us gave you a bottle of cognac anyway. And not bad cognac at that, Armenian cognac, four stars, maybe even KV. . . .

But let's forget our old offenses. Thank you for your company, Tadeusz Osipowicz. Regards to your wife. . . . Maybe we'll meet again. Who knows? By that time, I hope all the old apartment houses will be torn down and new ones up to take their place. I hope the Negroes will have moved out of the slums and into better housing. And I hope there will be just slightly fewer Columbuses. By the way, I've heard that the guidebooks tell you just where all the statues are and who they're built to. . . .

I've kept this last conversation especially for the end. It took place on the outskirts of New York, where there are no skyscrapers or advertising signs, near Lexington Avenue and One hundred and twenty-fifth Street, in a little bar not far from the Harlem River.

It was my last evening in America, and I wanted to spend it alone. I stepped out of my hotel and walked across Broadway: it was already almost empty. I walked as far as Grand Central, and went down into the subway. I decided to ride uptown for ten stops, and I got out at One hundred and twenty-fifth Street.

Past eleven. There is no one in the street. It is dark, a little like Tversky-Yamsky Street in Moscow. Street lights here and there, and fences. I am walking wherever my eyes are taking me. On the corner of two narrow streets I come to a small bar. It, too, is almost empty. At a table in the far corner, two unshaven men in blue overalls are drinking beer. Behind the bar, against a backdrop of many colored bottles, stands a very pretty Negro girl. On this side, facing her, two fellows lean against the bar: one in a leather jacket, the other, a Negro, in a bright checkered shirt. They are talking to the Negro girl, quietly. There is music playing, jazz, syncopated.

I walk up to the bar, put down a dollar, and raise one finger. Without interrupting her conversation, the Negro girl pours me a whiskey. I take it over to an empty table near the window, and then I go back for a glass of light beer and a small ham sandwich.

Here I am, sitting at a table, drinking beer and smoking a "Belomor." I can't spend any money on American cigarettes: I have to save enough for the subway. No one is paying any attention to me. The two men in overalls pay up and leave. The other two are still at the bar, talking. I look at the posters hung around—advertisements for White Horse Whiskey, Martini & Rossi, Coca-Cola. I am sitting alone in a bar on the outskirts of New York, drinking. If Ivan Ivanovich knew . . .

The Negro in the checkered shirt says good night and leaves. The other fellow lingers at the bar, counting his money. Then he orders another beer, and looking around the room, he comes to sit down at my table. Behind him, the girl wipes off the bar.

He's not a young man. He has gray hair at his temples and deep creases around his mouth. He smokes and drinks his beer without a word. Suddenly he looks at me, and he seems surprised.

"Belomor?" he says.*

"Yes, Belomor."

I hold out my pack and tap the bottom for him.

"I'm Lieutenant Patrick Stanley," he says. "Flying Fortress. Gunner-radioman. Poltava airfield."

* A brand of Soviet cigarette with a long paper mouthpiece which would make it immediately recognizable. (*Translator's note*)

We order two more.

Patrick Stanley, Flying Fortress, Poltava airfield. So it turns out that you and I have fought a war together. You in the air and I on the ground. And now we are sitting on the outskirts of New York drinking beer. You have good beer. It's strong and cold. . . . What are you laughing at? . . . You prefer vodka? You're right. Where did you learn to drink it? In our country, in the hospital? No, in the hospital you learned to drink straight alcohol. The nurses brought it to you—admit it. I was in the hospital, too. You were in Poltava, and I was in Baku. So that's the way it is. It's been seventeen years. And what do you do now. Fix TV sets. That's a good job.

Good job or not, I don't have enough money. Anyway, I guess no one ever has enough. Millionaires don't have enough either. But I have a son. He's seventeen years old, and he says he needs a car. You can buy a used one for two or three hundred, a pretty good one, too; but he has to have a new one. He quit school, the idiot, and now he has a job in a store. Why go to school, he says, when you can make money without it?

Is that right? I just got a letter from a friend of mine in Australia, and her son says the same thing. "Why go to school, when you can get a job . . . ?" Well, young people are always a problem. But I guess fathers always criticize their sons. Not that way, not that way either. We say we were never like that.

Yes, I guess we were really just the same. Well, let's have another beer. No, it's on me; I'm the host here. When I come to Russia, you can pay. . . . Yes, I'd love to go to Russia. I'll get some cash together, and my wife and I will come to Poltava. Well, no, maybe I should come alone.

There was a nurse named Klava in the hospital, I might run into her. No, I'd better come alone, don't you think? And on my way to Kiev, I'll stop to visit you. What kind of work do you do there? . . . Architect? Not bad. You must make some pretty good money if you can come here, here and back by plane. What do you say, just one more? . . . Don't look at us that way, Betsey. This is our last. We'll be leaving in a minute. . . . It's too bad your plane leaves tomorrow. You could spend the evening with us. See how an American like me lives. How do you like America? . . . No, only the truth. Our papers tell a lot of lies about you, but I don't believe them. What about yours? It's a shame, really. Who thought up this cold war anyway? We were friends while the hot one was on. Then when it was over, we started quarreling, and the cold one started. Who wants it? Do you? No, I know, you are good people. And we're not bad people either. Then what are we fighting about? Berlin. What do I care about Berlin? I certainly don't want to go to war over it. I've had enough fighting. And I don't want my son Jim to go to war over it either. I'd rather see him buy that car after all, let him take his girl for a ride in it. He's a great boy, he really is. It's too bad you have to go tomorrow. The three of us could go out together. Maybe we could get a bottle from Betsey now and go up to my place. My wife's away visiting her folks in Baltimore. . . . No, I guess not, I know you have to leave, and I have to get up early in the morning. It's too bad you won't see Jim, you'd like him. He even knows some Russian: *sputnik, lunnik, davay-davay, vodka.* He's a good boy. . . . No, he doesn't drink yet. Well, just a little when he's with his friends. My boy's an athlete, a hockey player, and a good swimmer. . . . We're going, Betsey, we're going.

You can close up now. Just remember today's date—the first time you ever had a Russian in your place. It doesn't happen every day.

The streets were empty. We hated to say good-by, so we walked down together to the next subway station. The subway runs all night.

Ah, Patrick, Patrick. Seventeen years ago you and I were fighting together, you in the air and I on the ground, and now we are marching late at night along the echoing streets of New York. It's good to be together and we hate to say good-by. And yet, for some reason our countries are not on friendly terms. Why is that? You and Jim must pay us a visit. We won't spend much time in museums, but we will show you some good fellows. I'll take you away from your tourist group, and we'll drive over to see one of my friends. He and I were in the same hospital in Baku, and now he's an electric welder. You don't know how happy he'll be to meet you and Jim, not because you're Americans, but because you're good men. And he's a good man, too. You'll like each other right away. He'll show off for you a little (good men or not, you're still Americans and he'll want to put on a good show for you). He'll turn on his television set for you, play up his wife and daughters a little, play me up, and his other friends, and his job. And then those friends of his will all come over, and we'll run down to the delicatessen before it closes, and there'll be a shower of questions, and everyone will be slapping you and Jim on the back. (And my friends have a pretty heavy hand.) And then Jim and one of the younger fellows will put their elbows on the table and get hold of each other's palms, and then everyone will be shouting, "Come on boy, do your stuff!" And everyone will be yelling and laughing and singing songs. And then at about three in the morning we'll look for a taxi and won't be able to find one, and we won't be too steady on our feet, and then we'll start wandering around Kiev late at night, just as we're doing now in New York, only there'll be more of us. Someone is bound to start up a chorus of "Do the Russians want war?" * And you and Jim will shout the answer, "The Americans don't want it either!" We'll have a good time together, and just like now, we'll hate to say good-by.

The trains run infrequently at this hour. Near a chewing-gum machine someone is sleeping on a bench. A Negro in blue overalls is sweeping the platform. It's already 2:00 A.M. Poor Ivan Ivanovich.

The train arrives. "Good-by, Patrick. Say hello to Jim for me."

I step into a car. The train moves. The train goes into a tunnel.

We flew from New York to Brussels in six and a half hours, without landing in Manchester or Shannon.

First the lights of New York disappeared, and then the stripe of lights set wider apart along the shore. Then they brought us supper. And now, we sit back and try to go to sleep. The overhead lights are switched off, and on the ceiling, artificial constellations are glowing quietly.

I can't get to sleep. I'm too tired out by everything I've seen in the past two weeks. And I can't sleep because I think of the fact that I'm flying over the Atlantic Ocean. Do you remember the wonderful film, *Stowaway in the Sky?* That's the way to fly over America and France, around the whole world. Not in a spaceship above the atmosphere, but just as in Lamorisse's film, with an eccentric grandfather and

* A popular Soviet antiwar song with lyrics by Yevgeny Yevtushenko. (*Translator's note*)

189

his grandson, at a height of a hundred and fifty feet, over forests and meadows, castles and cathedrals, steering around the towers of the Notre Dame, between factory chimneys and past the sheer cliffs of the Mont Blanc, over the English Channel, the Côte d'Azur. Then land in some village where they are just having a wedding, or on the tiny square of some provincial town. . . . Then take off again, billowing smoke through weird trumpets, like the Archangel Gabriel's. Flying, flying, rocking gently, in the antediluvian basket.

I lie back and think.

I think of what I saw and what I didn't get a chance to see, about the enormous country which I barely touched, about the skyscrapers of New York, about Dimitry Korinetz, about the steel-works department in the Ford Plant in Dearborn where I suddenly had the feeling I was in our own "Red October Plant" in Stalingrad. (I remembered what that had been like in '42 when the front lines passed right through it: dreadful, annihilated.) I thought about my argument with Volodya, about the six Marines raising the flag on Iwo Jima, about Patrick Stanley. . . .

Patrick Stanley. Flying Fortress. Gunner-radioman. How sorry I am that I did not manage to meet you, that this whole story of the trip late at night, the beautiful Negro girl, the pack of Belomors, is something I invented. There was no bar, no Negro girl, there was no Patrick. I only wish there had been.

I wish we really had sat in that little bar and thought back over the war we fought together. I wish we had had those drinks, and wandered around the streets at night. I wish there really had been a Jim somewhere, a good fellow even though he didn't want to study. (And there are Jims like that, there are. . . .) I wish he and his father would come to Kiev. We would all go over to my friend's house, and sing songs there, and then we would all walk together along the stilly streets of Kiev. Past Goloseyev Woods, down Red Army Street, and the Kreshchatik, down to the Dnieper, and there, sitting on the hills, we would watch the sun come up. . . . How I wish, how I wish we could.

On the ceiling, the constellations have gone out now. The stewardess walks quietly up the aisle. She looks pretty in her blue cap.

"We are flying over Paris. Brussels in one hour."

Through the porthole, it is getting light. You can't see a thing: clouds, unbroken clouds. It must be raining over Europe.

In two days, Moscow. Snow and light frost. And friends. There they stand, waving their caps.

"Welcome!"

In a moment the hugs and kisses will begin. And then the questions. Questions, questions, a hundred thousand of them. And they'll all have to be answered. It isn't easy. . . .